D0566074

DATE DUE

f
DT
56
G6613

EGYPT
OBSERVED

HENRI GOUGAUD AND COLETTE GOUVION

Translated from the French by Stephen Hardman

KAYE & WARD · LONDON

OXFORD UNIVERSITY PRESS · NEW YORK

First published by Librairie Hachette 1977
First published in Great Britain by Kaye & Ward Ltd
21 New Street, London EC2M 4NT
1979
First published in the USA by Oxford University Press Inc.
200 Madison Avenue, New York, NY 10016
1979

All rights reserved. No part of this publication may be
reproduced, stored in a retrieval system, or transmitted,
in any form or by any means, electronic, mechanical,
photocopying, recording or otherwise, without
the prior permission of the copyright owner.

ISBN 0 7182 1004 2 (Great Britain)
ISBN 0-19-520132-9 (USA)
Library of Congress Catalog Card Number 78-65869 (USA)
Printed in Italy by Mondadori, Verona

CONTENTS

INTRODUCTION

Doors and Keys   4

1. STROLLING THROUGH CAIRO

Cairo   10
The crowds of Cairo   14
The mosques of Cairo   20

2. THE CAIRO OF THE PHARAOHS

The Cairo Museum   28
The gods of ancient Egypt   31
Tutankhamun   33
The animal gods   34
The Pharaohs   38
Nut and Anubis   40
The Cairo Museum   43
The Sphinx and the Pyramids   45
The Pyramids of Giza   46

3. FROM CAIRO TO TELL EL AMARNA

Sakkara   48
Memphis   56
Wadi Natrun   59
Going up the Nile   62
Tell el Amarna   64
Towards Luxor   66

4. FROM TELL EL AMARNA TO LUXOR

Dendera   70
Karnak   72
Luxor   74
The Theban necropolis   76
Egypt ancient and modern   80
The Theban necropolis   82

5. FROM LUXOR TO ABU SIMBEL

From Esna to Aswan   90
Aswan   92
In Nubia   96
Abu Simbel   98

6. FROM SUEZ TO ALEXANDRIA

The Sinai   104
Siwa   106
The Delta   108
Alexandria   110
At the end of the journey   116

MAP   118

INFORMATION

The longest history in History   120
Egypt in the west   123
Advice from an Egyptian   127

INTRODUCTION

DOORS AND KEYS

— *Tell me my name.*
— *Shadow is your name.*
— *Tell me my name.*
— *He who leads the Great Goddess, this is your name.*
— *Tell me my name.*
— *He who knows the desert, he who lives amid the flowers, he who lives in the olive tree, this is your name.*

Book of the Dead

There are magical countries whose very names reach towards a dream world beyond the setting sun. The doorway leading to them is an invisible temple built in the mind of the traveller by mythical beings, and their last frontier post lies outside all geographical confines. Such a country is Egypt. It is bounded by a gold scarab at the threshold of the world and by a sphinx at the threshold of death; it is traversed by a fertile serpent, engendering life, and is inhabited by legend. But who gave it its roots? 'A people that pushes the water with their feet', as the Bible says, a powerful sun in a perfect sky, a rich and majestic river, the Nile. Once the traveller has passed through the door of myth, he is confronted by water, real fire, flesh and vegetation. A first and a primary truth is established: magic Egypt is a human land.

Of a total area of nine hundred thousand square kilometres, fields and towns occupy thirty-four thousand and barren sand and bare rock cover eight hundred and fifty-six thousand square kilometres. The population numbers thirty-six millions, nine hundred and seventy-five to the square kilometre. This is where the paradoxes begin. This country is the most empty and the most fertile, the most plentiful, the most disconcerting, the most desert-bound in North East Africa and the largest oasis in the world. Here the longest civilization of Antiquity was born. Here truths contradict one another, images are piled one on another without ever losing their identity. Here the shadows have their own shadows. About 1940 a minister, Hefni Mahmud Pasha, wanted to have the mirages that haunt the road from Alexandria to Cairo classified as historic monuments. He was right. In Egypt the great beauty spots are of intangible stone, history is conjugated in the past-present tense and speech navigates a course between an unreal violence and a genuine pacifism, mocking but courteous, profound but frivolous, melancholy but serene.

The Nile.

An Egyptian and his son.

It is said that, three thousand two hundred years before Christ, the legendary King Menes unified the two kingdoms in a single state, the North devoted to the cult of Osiris and the South to that of the god Set. No-one has ever reversed his decree. Occupying this indivisible land, however, four successive peoples have been distinguished by the geographers of the times. The Egypt of the Pharaohs asserts itself with the power of the colossi, but it remains forever as impalpable, as inaccessible as any vanished civilization. It existed for at least forty centuries — twice as long as the period dating from the dawn of Christianity. It was the mother of all the Mediterranean civilizations, of agriculture, architecture, the major techniques and arts. In short, says Ibrahim Fahri, it 'invented God, the cultivation of the fava bean, secret writing and pictorial representation, the functions and habits of the soul' — life, in a word. That Egypt died, its tomb sealed by Cleopatra VII — the only known Cleopatra, loved by Caesar.

Among the temples and the gardens came strange Christians, a turbulent and scholarly body of men. At Alexandria, the favourite city of the philosophers, a crucible bubbling with ideas at this beginning of a new era, some were Gnostics, believing that study and knowledge provided a better path to God than simple faith. Others founded the Coptic Church, which was by no means militant. Today there still remain Coptic monasteries, monuments, above all a splendid, sensitive, sad and strangely modern art, and five million faithful.

From the end of the Roman occupation the Christians lived among the sons of Allah, who gave the East this African country where Europe soon established its influence. Muslim Egypt had its periods of excess, like every country in the world. But in the Middle Ages it was powerful, studious and refined. Its literature, passionately interested in the art of living and thinking, preserved the finest part of the Greek heritage. Its princes were great men, among them Saladin who vanquished the Crusaders. Its architects were experts: the mosques of Ibn Tulun and Hassan, the University of El Azhar were their glorious achievement. They still exert a firm hold on the heart of modern Egypt, which honours their memory and feeds on their knowledge.

Times have changed, however. This very old and venerable country was a Civilization with a capital C. Today it is a 'developing country' and of an almost impudent youthfulness: the average age of its thirty-six million inhabitants is twenty-seven, and one Egyptian in two is under twenty. Now Egypt, despite its faults and creakings, is hailed as the leading industrial nation in the Middle East and the queen of cotton. It is growing and strengthening its muscles. The Aswan dam has been built, agrarian reform organized, and the fertile lands distributed to the peasants. Wars smoulder, burst into flame and are extinguished. The population is increasing

Threshing wheat in a village near Cairo.

rapidly; housing is still inadequate and food is still too meagre. The people still live on hope, but their hearts are strong and their souls remain strangely rich in a knowledge without words.

A moment of ordinary life is glimpsed as one passes: at the foot of the pyramids, near a fruit stall surrounded by flies, an old man is sitting on the edge of a pavement. He is dressed in a dusty *galabieh* (cotton robe) and a tattered turban. His eyes sparkle from a face riddled with lines. In the full heat of the sun he is dreaming. On the pavement opposite a tourist stops and aims his camera at him. The old man catches sight of the tourist and makes the impatient gesture of someone annoyed by an insect. The tourist insists. The man puts his hands over his face and does not budge. He refuses to be photo-graphed, for he does not want his real face to be stolen from him and appear like a fake against a background of sky. He mistrusts images devoid of vitality.

As the traveller sets out on his journey he should think of this old man with gratitude, for he possesses a simple and precious truth: all that matters is life as it is lived. One should beware there-fore of going to Egypt as if one were going to the cinema, armed with childish notions fostered by school books, Hollywood Cleo-patras, coloured sphinxes against a desert backdrop and museum souvenirs. And to make sure of starting with a truly open mind, forget all about any rigid preconceptions. Israel, the Arabs, Suez and Port Said are newspaper words. One realizes this as soon as the first

The University of Cairo.

face is seen, the first look exchanged, the first word heard in the first street you set foot on in Cairo. Egypt is first and foremost inhabited by human beings, a fact worth observing about a country where the only true ghettos are those which tourists themselves erect around their travels. So you must go and meet the real people. But do not hope to gain any clear-cut knowledge or certitude. Life is not amenable to fixed ideas. You will never force the secret of half glimpsed mysteries.

The Word, however, is all powerful in Egypt. There is no other country where a greeting is so friendly, a word of love so tender, an insult so brutal, or a curse so final. The Egyptians know by instinct the exorcizing power of discussion; it frees them from the need of the aggressive gesture, and, moreover, it nourishes a pacifism that is deeply rooted in their consciousness. To invest love and friendship with precious words, to insult in order not to have to fight — is this simply the Eastern way of things, or is it peculiarly Egyptian? The ancient riverside dwellers of the Nile inscribed these two sentences

in hieroglyphics before the Bible existed: 'The Word creates everything, all that we love and hate, the totality of being. Nothing exists before it has been uttered in a clear voice.' These men possessed such powers of incantation that they made statues talk, writes Kurt Seligman in a strange book entitled *Mirror of Magic*: 'The sphinxes opened their mouths of stone and revealed the will of the gods. The Fathers of the Christian Church bear explicit witness to the fact that these statues could speak. Often the king and his assembled people attended this sort of oracle, and the scribes wrote down what was said on their papyrus.'

This art is lost to the world, but words still fascinate, magnifying life and filling it with a sense of wonder. 'Your absence has made me wild', says the Egyptian to a returning friend — a cordial welcome in the strictest sense of the term, for the heart beats in these words. Moreover, in this country it could be said that a heart beats in all things, even in the sun which was named, blessed and implored like a god and tenderly loved like a human father, and even in the dark stone of the tombs. The sturdy peasant carved four thousand years ago on the wall of the house of a dead man, at Sakkara, can be encountered at a roadside, driving his buffaloes under the palm-trees. Along the Nile you will see women carrying pitchers of water on their heads; their exact likeness was also engraved on the wall of a temple four thousand years ago. You will discover human pro-files carved on the wall of a royal tomb and will recognize them both in the university amphitheatres and among the crowds at the Ramesses station, against a background of suitcases and bundles of clothes. A child will come towards you among the oranges at the Khan el Khalili market, a crafty, chattering child, a poor child with an expression that is restless, lively, anxious, smiling, solemn, mock-ing, attentive and tireless. As you watch him, all mirages banished, you will contemplate the indefinable reality and will finally under-stand these words of André Malraux: 'The Egypt which first in-vented eternity is also the most powerful actress in life.' So do not set out with the intention of discovering this country. It is Egypt which, by your good fortune, will take possession of you.

Nasser's funeral in Cairo, 1st October 1970.

I

STROLLING THROUGH CAIRO

The storyteller of ancient times, sitting sheltered from the wind, refers to a place known by the man listening to him: 'At this place where the oasis turns into dust', he says, 'the phoenix burns every evening on a pyre of myrrh and incense to be reborn from its ashes at dawn.' Later, on this stretch of land exalted by legend, Heliopolis ('City of the Sun') was built. Today only the name survives: Heliopolis is now an airport built at the place once occupied by the phoenix and the dazzling city, a magnificent gateway of the imagination through which the traveller passes as he leaves the aeroplane to discover **Cairo**, the meeting place of all the phases of Egyptian history.

The airport cannot claim to be architecturally inspiring, but in the daytime it smells warm and good. At night it is covered by a myriad stars unknown below the mists of Europe, a soothing, pure sky. In its enormous reception hall you are constantly confronted with the most beautiful scenes on earth — human faces; sharp-witted children, brown, black or white; peaceable soldiers walking in a leisurely fashion and holding their rifles like a shepherd's crook; women with sunny, touching expressions, dressed in Western or Eastern style, or half-way between the two; bustling silhouettes carefully dressed in *galabiehs*, *burnous* and *tarbooshes*; swarthy men with a lively eye, a perpetual smile and chattering volubly. The French poet Gérard de Nerval, who visited Egypt over a hundred years ago, summed up this colourful and kindly humanity in these words: 'The people here are wonderfully gentle. They would be the best people on earth if it was not for their greed for the *bashiz* [tip].' Nothing, it seems, has changed.

But to sum up a people is really to say nothing. The traveller should not set out, armed with reason, hoping fully to understand either Cairo or its people. It would be better to mobilize the five senses and the unsophisticated child who exists within all of us, to listen to the noise of the crowd, its cries, its talk, its music, to watch for all the countless gestures and the outward signs of life, to smell the air, enjoy the weather and contemplate the eternal city walls. Throughout history many have immersed themselves in this city, have become intoxicated and have been unable to forget it. Nerval, Flaubert, Maxime Du Camp, Théophile Gautier, Chateaubriand, Bonaparte, the Franciscan friars who in the sixteenth century accompanied the first French ambassadors, before them the Crusaders — all were captivated by this dusky, carefree capital where no-one has ever succeeded in distinguishing the immutable from the daily routine of life.

Cairo seen from the top of the minaret of the mosque of Ibn Tulun. In the foreground the college built in 1356 by the emir El Serghatmach.

The Nile and the islands of Rodah (foreground) and Gezira.

From the airport to the metropolis the road runs straight between the houses of the new Heliopolis. In 1905 a Belgian, Baron Empain, decided to erect a new city on the site of the sacred Heliopolis. Among the gardens and the palm trees he built a sort of Neo-Moorish 'Belle Époque' Brussels and a bewildering palace, a kind of Cambodian temple adorned with Arab architecture and Walloon imagination. Today Empain's folly passes quickly from behind the windows of the taxis going into the city, eagerly racing past red lights in a din of blaring hooters, skilfully winding their way among unexpected bicycles, wobbling carts, asses plodding their way since time immemorial, and daydreaming pedestrians. Immediately the visitor is confronted with the inextricable tangle which is Cairo. The noise of machines interspersed with human cries, laughter, gleaming cars and loaded beasts, merchants, beggars, students, slow-moving women, ageless old men, squealing children, half-naked or fancily dressed, gold and dirt, cheap finery and strictly correct costume, dust and sun, bright colours and a warm mist — everything mingling and moving in crowds along a maze of straight avenues, esplanades, alleys dotted with mosques, brief glimpses of the Nile, small, silent squares where sometimes a tread-mill turns, enamelled in green and red. 'There is a light here which one only sees as a child, with fresh eyes,' said Gérard de Nerval. It is true, the light is marvellous. But it is not a light seen by the geographers.

Yet one must attempt a topographical reconaissance of this labyrinth. Like all the cities on the banks of the Nile, Cairo is built on the narrow fertile strip that divides the sea of sand in two. In the river lie two islands, **Rodah** and **Gezira**, green havens of peace. To the south east is the rocky Arab hill, the Mukattam, stripped bare by the desert wind. Built onto the Mukattam is the formidable citadel erected by Saladin, its ochre walls rising into the blue sky. Below the citadel lies **Old Cairo**, a district swarming with endlessly twisting alleys, mosques, cemeteries, the market of Khan el Khalili, packed with people, carts, sheep, donkeys, camels, fruits, tea, liquors and meat, the scents of amber, the smell of leather and dung, the whiffs of cooking, the gaudy reds and the pastels shimmering in the dusty heat. In the direction of the Nile the European quarters were erected during the nineteenth and twentieth centuries. They have proliferated wildly and today almost surround the pyramids. Between the old and the new Cairo lies the area intended to be the heart of the city, Midan el Tahrir ('Liberation Square'). Here is to be found the gleaming Hilton with its high glass doors, and from

Old Cairo.

A street in Old Cairo.

The crowd in Cairo.

the square the Egyptian Museum extends to Shari el Galaa, a wide avenue leading to the Ramesses station.

This is the district that the visitor first discovers, and it offers little of interest. Straight up-and-down modern blocks, straight avenues, elegant cars, cinemas and neon lighting, international hotels with voluptuous carpets and the heavy crockery of a railway restaurant car, everything could belong to some other city. On Qasr el Nil Street the cafés are French, the shops English, the banks nationalized but like banks all over the world. The bridge leading to Gezira, El Tahrir, is flanked by two British lions and would not look out of place on the Thames. We are in Cairo, capital of the Middle East, and all capitals resemble each other in some way. One might say that they all know each other, that they belong to the same British club, a little stiff-necked, political, polyglot, modern, design conscious, but not lacking a comfortable charm. If one is not an inveterate seeker of the exotic one can, in European Cairo, spend a while cultivating the habits of a British major and amuse oneself in a dignified manner, without extravagance but with enthusiasm and moderation. One can have a drink at the Café Vert on Qasr el Nil Street, passing on the way the enormous façade of the offices of *Al-Ahram*, the largest daily newspaper in the Arab world.

To discover what lies behind the outward appearance, however, all one needs to do is to climb to the top floor of one of the drab modern blocks and look out of the highest window. Then you will find yourself gazing down onto the low roofs of the neighbouring buildings and the inner courtyards, discovering a hotchpotch of metal sheeting erected among the straw and wood. Washing can be

seen drying between the wrecks of two cars hoisted onto a flat roof by some impoverished magician, half starved figures threading their way among swaying scaffolding and leaking cisterns, calling to one another and, crouched in front of miserable fires, cooking a meagre meal. Behind the Western décor, the East wears no make-up and is not acting a part. It is living. Then you know for sure that you are passing through a theatre and that the real, raw world lies beyond. You can stroll again, without being taken in, along the gracious stage where every effort has been made to offer the traveller a smooth journey. In the district of the large hotels, where you will no doubt be staying, you will find that they are all on the bank of the Nile. The Semiramis, with its famous restaurant the 'Night and Day', once the plush rendezvous of journalists and senior officials, is no more. However, there is still the Shepheards and the Hilton, a little further along Midan el Tahrir, which provides, without modesty but also without fuss, for the luxury world of the businessman and the dollar-rich on holiday. A visit to the bar on the eighteenth floor is strongly recommended, even if only to spend a lazy evening, with a background of sweet music, relishing the marvellous panorama of the city from the windows.

Along the Nile runs the Corniche, the revolution's gift to the city. Crossing the bridge with the two lions (El Tahrir), you come onto Gezira ('the fresh island'), where British associations persist: the Sporting Club with its golf course and swimming-pool, once the centre of social life and now a stubborn witness to a time that people would like forgotten. Nowadays the inhabitants of Cairo love to invade Gezira when in a festive mood. On Friday, the

By tram.

weekly day of rest, on the occasion of the Great Bairam (tenth day after the Ramadan) or the Shamm en Nessim (the spring festival), they put on their best clothes and flock to this beautiful place. They take over the Corniche, the Sporting Club, the gardens and the smooth lawns. They crowd round the itinerant vendors and their multicoloured little cars which are also decked out in their Sunday best, they consume enormous piles of tomato macaroni, steaming lentils, *baladi* salad, grilled brochettes, syrups, ices and fruit juices of every colour. They laugh, sing, shout, guzzle, play games and lose their children in the dense crowd which only a few daring acrobats perched on bicycles dare to penetrate. Anyone who comes by car must abandon all hope of finding a way through: he will be engulfed in the throng like a ship sinking at sea. The easy going policemen (*shaouish*) of Cairo know this full well and go off to drink lemonade, happily let themselves be captivated by an open-air show of shrill, exotic marionettes, go with the crowd to watch the **strolling players'** entertainment where the female roles are often taken by men in make-up, and then stroll about at the firework display held on the Corniche. When night comes, everyone makes his way slowly home along the wide pavements of El Tahrir bridge, the women in front holding their varnished shoes in their hands, their feet free at last on the lukewarm cement, the men behind carrying on their shoulders their weary children, intoxicated with the hubbub and the colours.

For every festival has its own colour. The Great Bairam is violent pink, the pink of the sign carved on the fleeces of the sheep who will be slaughtered and eaten on that day, the pink of the linen wrapped round their flesh displayed on the butchers' stalls at the markets and along the streets. Shamm en Nessim is green with flowers everywhere. It is the most beautiful festival in Egypt and the most ancient, for in the time of the Pharaohs the 'breeze of spring' was already welcomed as a time for rejoicing. It celebrates the renewal of the earth, when the corn comes out and the lambs are born. It is observed on the Monday of the Coptic Easter and is meant to be Arab and Muslim — in other words, spring is life itself, belongs to all and must be blessed by all. In Cairo it is joyfully celebrated. In the aristocratic quarters, among the gardens, people spread themselves out with their picnics, quench their thirst and devour mountains of glittering confectionery. Between Boulak and Gezira, *feluccas* with their white sails set, painted in various colours and decorated with streamers

Strolling players in the streets of Cairo.

flapping in the wind, pass slowly along the Nile. The spring boats pitch in the water, and birds hover above the masts in the pure sky. One can imagine oneself on a perfect Sunday, among the simple people, the innocent children and the universal symbols. On the lawns they offer sacrifice to the gods of the countryside: at breakfast they devour beans, hard-boiled eggs, small, fresh onions and the *fessikh*, the fish ritually eaten in sacrifice from time immemorial on the altar of fertility (do the merrymakers realize this?).

When the festival is over, the dignitaries and officials of Cairo can still be found wandering along the banks of the Nile, invading the luxury restaurants, savouring grilled pigeon (the national dish) and enjoying the freshness of the evening in the deserted gardens. For the people have returned to their dusty quarters — Bab el Sharia, Shubra, Boulak, Abdine, Sayeda Zeinab. The traveller should follow them, as this is the only way to discover the real Arab Cairo, ancient Cairo, historic Cairo, the irrational Cairo of dreams, wild, dirty, and wonderful as a fairy-tale. A religious traveller of the sixteenth century, Jehan Thenaud, said of this

The rose-seller.

Cairo: 'It is three times as big as Paris, and above it hover a hundred thousand kites which perfume it with their droppings.' In 1535 Greffin Affagart described his astonishment at 'this great and unparalleled city, its 14,000 parish churches, its very narrow, short streets mostly covered with vaulting because of the extreme heat of the summer . . .', its 20,000 kitchens, its vendors of minced meat 'cooked in small pieces like larks', its 5,000 water-carriers with their goatskin bottles, the houses' marble paving 'arranged in the Venetian fashion with singular art'. Where is this medieval Cairo? Vanished in the passage of time? No, it is still there, unchanged. Its poverty, first of all, cannot escape the eye. In Cairo one understands what density of population

Apples.

means. Only in India would one find so many people in such a small area: the labyrinths of Bab el Sharia number one hundred and twelve thousand inhabitants to the square kilometre, and the popular quarters on average sixty thousand. What kind of people inhabit these places? Some are natives of Cairo, but masses of exiled peasants have flocked to the big city desperately seeking

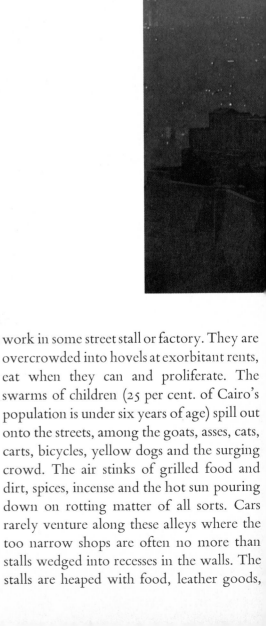

work in some street stall or factory. They are overcrowded into hovels at exorbitant rents, eat when they can and proliferate. The swarms of children (25 per cent. of Cairo's population is under six years of age) spill out onto the streets, among the goats, asses, cats, carts, bicycles, yellow dogs and the surging crowd. The air stinks of grilled food and dirt, spices, incense and the hot sun pouring down on rotting matter of all sorts. Cars rarely venture along these alleys where the too narrow shops are often no more than stalls wedged into recesses in the walls. The stalls are heaped with food, leather goods,

The mosque of Mehemet Ali and the citadel.

grey, brown and unbleached garments, and an incongruous medley of crockery. The only signs of the twentieth century that one is likely to come across in the course of a random stroll might be a portrait of President Nasser in a basket of dazzling oranges, a transistor radio in a basket of tomatoes, or a ray of sun shining on a magazine film star pinned next to a thermometer in a tailor's shop. Behind them the history of Cairo from the time of the Romans pursues its imperturbable course. But to relate this history clearly one must leave the clutter of the medieval city.

In the time of the Pharaohs, on the right bank of the Nile opposite the island of Rodah, stood a village, or perhaps a city: Kheri Aha ('place of the combat'). There, according to a myth, Set-of-the-Night and Horus-the-Light engaged in combat in primeval times. Today the site is occupied by Garden City, the fashionable district. On the island of Rodah, on the site of the Manyal Palace (Club Méditerranée) once stood Per Hapi en Iun ('the house of the Nile'). Rodah and Kheri Aha probably formed part of Heliopolis. When the Greeks came they called the place 'Babylon in Egypt' (perhaps

The voice of the muezzin.

teapot in his hand. The houses are small and simple, with narrow windows and a single shutter that is sometimes fastened back. A woman appears and calls. We might almost be wandering through the daily world of the Middle Ages, inhabited by gentle, silent people. Since its very first morning this world seems not to have budged an inch. No sign of modern times, no electric cable clutters the ochre, pale blue or white walls, or the pavement where there hardly seems to be any dust. Now and again one must bend one's head as one passes beneath a vaulted roof from one alley to another, looking for the churches which do not always have the obvious features of a church and can hardly be distinguished from the adjoining houses. Yet they are all there, their names forming a strange litany, and as one passes through the discreet thresholds one has the feeling of penetrating the heart of a wise man. The church of

In the mosque of Mehemet Ali.

their distortion of Per Hapi en Iun). Then the Romans arrived and fortified Babylon. About 30 BC Augustus erected a fortress which was to be rebuilt twice, by Trajan and by the Christian emperor Arcadius. A few traces of the fortress can still be seen. It was next the turn of the Copts, who had come to Christianity by obscure paths, no doubt influenced by the disputations of the Alexandrian philosophers. Three centuries later they made a pact with the Muslims who proved highly tolerant, leaving them quite free to build churches. Nearly all these churches lie within the enclosure walls of the former Babylon, which the conquering Arabs named Qasr el Shamah (today Old Cairo), opposite the southern tip of the island of Rodah.

The best time to wander through the Coptic quarter is at night-fall. Children play quietly. An old man crosses the street, a steaming

The interior of the mosque of Mehemet Ali.

El Moallaqah ('the hanging church') is built on a bastion of the fortress; its nave covers the passage leading inside the rampart wall. The church of Abu Sarga (St Sergius) is one of the oldest in Cairo; according to the priest's sister who will tell you its story, the Holy Family passed through its crypt. The church of Sitt Barbara (St Barbara) is said to have been built by a wealthy scribe named Athanasius in 684. Then you come to El Adrah and Mari Girgis (St George's), and the cloister of St Theodore the Oriental, the high wall of which encloses two churches, Abu Kir (St Cyrus) and St John. The Deir Abu Sefein was the monastery of St Mercurius. Inside the walls of Deir Mari Mina (the monastery of St Menas) is one of the oldest churches in the world, if in fact it was built in the fifth century.

Most of these churches are built on the same basilican plan, with the narthex to the west. In the centre of the narthex, in the oldest churches, was a large, deep basin filled with holy water in which the faithful submerged themselves on the eve of the Epiphany. The nave, with columns along each side and surrounded by a gallery where formerly the women were accommodated, is bounded on the main entrance side by a second basin used on Maundy Thursday for the ceremony of the washing of the feet. The chancel extends across the whole width of the church. An iconostasis of elaborately carved wood, with a door in the centre closed by a curtain and flanked by two skylights, separates the sanctuary from the assembled congregation. On the front of the iconostasis the icons are aligned. In front of them lamps burn and ostrich eggs are placed.

Three chapels crowned with a dome usually occupy the sanctuary, each with an altar. Quite apart from the architecture, a wonderful sense of peace is conveyed by the many colours of the wood, and among the painted images the faithful tell visitors of their love of the Coptic language, the most ancient of the Egyptian dialects since the word 'Copt' is the Arabic transcription of the Greek word *egyptoi*. In fact, these Christians dating from such distant times are Egypt's oldest children.

Their storehouse of treasures, the Coptic Museum, is near the 'hanging church' (El Moallaqah). It is worth a long visit, for its collection of rare objects is quite fascinating. In a peaceful maze of inner courts and small gardens, among the fragrant panelling and the ancient *mushrabiyyah* (wooden lattices), is displayed the daily life, sacred and profane, of Egypt's Christian period. Between Antiquity and Islam, the acts of men and their inspired works are represented: manuscripts on papyrus, wood carvings, doors, iconostases, carved panels, icons, ivories and some masterpieces of fabric work. The oldest fabrics, woven from flax, originate from the Christian necropolises of Upper Egypt and date from the third century. They are of unusual beauty, noble and serene, and pervaded with the light of a delivered soul.

A few steps from St Sergius, in the shade of a garden, the ancient synagogue resembles the silent old man with the large forehead and melancholy expression who will guide you, his keys clanging on his wrist, to the precious manuscript known as the 'Atlas of Moses' and also to the very old Torah written on gazelle skin which is said to date from the fifth century BC. The Jewish community of Old Cairo, its roots buried deep in time, has survived every storm. Today

The mosque of El Azhar.

forty families live in poverty around their temple, like villagers around their parish church. Here no-one disturbs their peace. If anyone should wonder at seeing them live here without persecution, in spite of tensions and wars, and should ask some awkward question, any native of Cairo will reply proudly, and sometimes not without vehemence: 'The Jews who live in Egypt are Egyptians.' The synagogue is in the garden, the faithful in their synagogue, and peace in the hearts of the faithful, for Allah is great.

It is now time to leave this quiet haven and return to the Arab city with its throng, its mosques, its tall, thin houses and everything that aroused the admiration of the barbarians who came from the West in the Middle Ages. The gentle slope of history once again invites the traveller to make a detour towards the past, to the time when Copts and Arabs became acquainted. In 642 there appeared a first military leader, Amr ibn el As, general of the caliph Omar. He besieged and without any difficulty captured the Graeco-Roman-Coptic Babylon. Inside the walls of his camp he built a new city, Fustat ('the tent'). Houses with patios, mills and oil presses, cisterns, wells, water channels, sewers and even a church were constructed in this city, the foundations of which are still discernible to the north east of Qasr el Shamah. The enterprising general also founded a mosque, which has been so completely restored that nothing today remains of the old stones. As for the city, it was to undergo such large-scale development that it soon assumed the traditional name of Misr, which designated the whole of Egypt. The vigorous Fustat thus grew until 1168, when it was burned to prevent it from falling into the hands of the besieging Crusaders. With the passage of time Egypt came under the rule of the Ommayyads from Damascus, the Abbasids from Baghdad, the Tulunids, the Ikhshidids and others. All these princes were duped: as soon as a governor general found himself on the banks of the Nile, he forgot

Old Arab house: Gayer-Anderson Museum.

his distant master, seized power for himself and built endlessly. And so, from dynasty to dynasty, from true sultan to false caliph, Cairo acquired innumerable mosques. There are still five hundred standing.

The proudest of these pious usurpers was undoubtedly Ahmed ibn Tulun. In 868 he abandoned Fustat, installed himself on the foothills of the Mukattam, built the district of El Katai and erected the mosque which today is the oldest and most spacious of all, and which bears his name, Ibn Tulun. It is built of bricks, the walls, pillars and arches are dressed with engraved stucco, and an immense enclosure wall, flanked by a parapet walk, surrounds it. The harmony of this building testifies to the fact that this man's reign was not one of vanity. He was enlightened, cultivating knowledge and wisdom; it was he who succeeded in integrating the Arab culture with the Graeco-Egyptian heritage.

The years passed and with them the conquerors. A century later, in 969, the caliph of Kairwan, El Muizz, sent his general Jawhar to conquer Egypt. Jawhar conquered, founded a city and named it El Qahira ('the victorious') on the day when the planet Mars (El Qahir) was passing above his head while the foundations of the enclosure walls were being dug. The Kheri Aha of Pharaonic times and Jawhar's El Qahira thus provide the twin etymologies of the name 'Cairo'. Jawhar continued to build; **El Azhar** (p. 22) was his work, copied from a former Byzantine basilica in Damascus which had been converted into a mosque. It is the greatest centre of Muslim theology in the Arab world. All Muslim Egyptian intellectuals have studied here, from the richest citizen to the poorest peasant sent by the *imam* of his village. Nowadays its teaching programme has been modernized; new subjects are included and a new section caters for students. Twenty-five thousand young people attend the university, among them quite a large number of foreigners

The interior of the Saleh Talai mosque.

attracted by its prestige. Its courses are free, being financed by the Muslim religious foundations, the Waqfs. At one time the university provided stingy meals and poor accommodation for its students. They slept in stalls enclosed by *mushrabiyyahs*, in the shadow of the minarets. Now they receive a monthly allowance and rent rooms in the neighbouring districts. But El Azhar, 'the most flowering', remains an inspiring and an honoured institution, for it lives in powerful rhythm with the Koranic soul that gave it birth.

With the arrival of Jawhar, Cairo began to enjoy a long period of architectural splendour. In 1087 the Armenian vizir of the caliph El Moustansir enclosed the city with ramparts pierced with sixty fortified gates, three of which remain: Bab el Futtuh, Bab el Nasr and Bab Zuweila. Opposite the latter stands the **Saleh Talai mosque** dating from the same period (1160). Then came Saladin, who built the **citadel** (p. 19), on the Mukattam, and established the first college mosque in Egypt. When the Mameluks arrived they erected the Kalaum mosque and, in 1356, the *madrasah* (college) of Sultan Hassan. In death the Mameluks today reign over the City of the Dead, a strange place covered with mosques, minarets and tombs on the red slopes of the hill of Gabal Ahmar. The visitor should wander among the mausoleums — that of Qaitbai is a pure surrealist gem — with the crowd that comes on the days of the Mulud, on foot, on donkeys and on decorated bicycles, to picnic on the warm slabs and joyfully honour the dead. On returning from this land of phantoms, you should also go to marvel at the magnificence of the **mosque of Mehemet Ali** (pp. 19–21). Built in the nineteenth century by Mehemet Ali on the model of the mosques in Constantinople, it is covered entirely with alabaster. It only remains now to lose oneself in the lively bazaar of Khan el Khalili. The bazaar has probably not changed since Sultan Ashraf

Loudspeakers broadcasting the prayer of the muezzin.

el Khalil had it built in the thirteenth century. Here one is in the world of the Thousand and One Nights, a dazzling display of endless variety, illuminated by a gentle moon, perfumed with amber, spices and dung, packed with slow-moving men, rowdy children, animals, fruits, vegetables, leather and copper goods, Pharaonic bric-a-brac and tiny cafés where people go to drink tea and smoke the *narghileh*. The most curious of all is the Fishawi café, the haunt of

decadent intellectuals, crammed with tarnished mirrors, stuffed animals and ostrich eggs. The Khan el Khalili is one of the beating hearts of Cairo, the great city which you must explore with all your senses on the alert, and which you must quietly resign yourself to never understanding.

Then, when night comes, you can indulge your dreams. Climb the Mukattam and watch the crescent moon in the dark blue sky, the minarets encircled by stars.

2

THE CAIRO OF THE PHARAOHS

The pyramids, temples and tombs, enveloped in a light invisible to the uninspired eye, speak a language that one must learn. When Gérard de Nerval visited Egypt he realized this and wisely said: 'One must see each place only after having gained sufficient knowledge of it through books.' In his day the stones had hardly been awakened from their slumber. The library of the Egyptian Society was their memory. There they remembered and told of their past. The traveller listened to them, then went among the ruins, and his visit proved fruitful. He saw the aura surrounding the colossi of rock in the shimmering heat, he heard living shadows slip through the porticos, he saw half ruined dwellings transfigured in the blazing sun, and his excitement was unforgettable.

Today the memories of the stones, patiently restored to the world's awareness, are as abundant as life itself. There is no longer any need to go round the libraries. Sacred, profane, sometimes intimate, always astounding and infinitely precious, they are all — or nearly all — to be found on the bank of the Nile, to the north of the Midan el Tahrir, in an enormous T-shaped building with labyrinthine galleries: the **Egyptian Museum of Antiquities**. This place is probably without a rival. There is certainly no other museum in the world where one can gaze upon the faultless fresco of a civilization and trace its history straight from its birth in prehistoric times to its death in the Roman period.

The edifice erected about 1900 by the French architect Dourgnon has the heavy, comfortable appearance of a Parisian *pâtisserie*. On first sight one half expects a dreary tour past lifeless treasures and among glum schoolchildren. However, hardly has one entered the museum when the heart begins to beat wildly: this is the treasure house of a lost world, bathed in the bluey green light of an aquarium. Here lie thousands of fabulous objects that seem to possess some dream-like quality because of their very great age. At least a thousand are masterpieces. And the rest? A series of marvels, signs, imprints, gestures and faces belonging to a life beyond, faces at once too familiar and too remote, too beautiful and too dead not to have an oppressive, disturbing, even frightening effect. What were Howard Carter's feelings, on 4 November 1922, as he exhumed from a previously unviolated tomb the **treasure of Tutankhamun**, now on exhibition in the museum? Was he dumbfounded by the discovery and terrified by the sacrilege? Sometimes a tourist will faint when confronted with these impassive mummies. A thousand invisible doors open onto secrets perhaps too intimate in this museum which has been arranged somehow to deceive the soul,

'Tutankhamun massacring the Nubians'. Wooden casket covered with painted stucco. Egyptian Museum of Antiquities.

Sheikh el Beled.
Statue of painted wood.
Egyptian Museum of
Antiquities.

without the knowledge of the builders and the archaeologists.

Originally installed at Boulak, then at Giza, the Egyptian Museum was the creation of a Frenchman, Mariette, in 1858. Before him, a number of archaeologists had been clearing excavation sites that proved too rich ever to be harvested. The impetuous Baron Vivant Denon, a painter and writer, published in 1802 an illustrated account of the first *Journey into Lower and Upper Egypt during the campaigns of General Bonaparte*. Then the mission sent by the future emperor brought back in their boxes a pile of material whose publication took twenty-five years: the *Description of Egypt*, in nine volumes, a work that paved the way for the study of Egyptology. In 1830 Champollion, the decoder of hieroglyphs, drew up for Mehemet Ali the first inventory of the country's monuments. Mariette, for his part, discovered the Serapeum at Memphis (seven thousand pieces were dispatched to the Louvre) and four masterpieces of Pharaonic statuary: Chephren, the Crouching Scribe, Nufreh and the striking statue of **Sheikh el Beled**. The last named is a lifesize statue of painted wood; the eyes are set with quartz, rock-crystal and ebony. In fact, it really represents a dignitary by the name of Kaaper, a contemporary of Cheops. Mariette organized the excavations on a systematic basis, fought the plundering that was rampant during the nineteenth century, and in 1856 was appointed 'Mamur' of works and antiquities. He devoted his life to Egypt, and in gratitude Egypt honours his name.

The marvels displayed in his museum are surrounded by a labyrinthine network of passages that tempt the visitor to wander at random. Apart from the compulsory routes dictated by the guide, one may choose one's own itinerary according to whim, engaging in a friendly dialogue with some mummified princess with an inscrutable look, humbly trying to discover the secret of life

Predynastic clay statuette.
Egyptian Museum of Antiquities.

from some grains of wheat which have survived three thousand years of slumber and which — according to a touching legend — would still be capable of germinating if sown in the soil, or day-dreaming before the **clay statuette** (p. 29) **of a fertile mother** who seems never to have ceased, since the predynastic era, to nurture her children with pure art.

As you roam round the museum you must remain on the alert, for everything here speaks without words: a servant girl and a workman, a spoon, a comb, a piece of fabric, a press and a bread oven; countless objects telling of the simple life, daily work, the activities and the little pleasures of a very remote people who suddenly, by some miracle, appear to be in your presence; the **falcon Horus**, god of the Sun, with its dazzling eyes. Like the sky which arches over the tree, here solemn thought is to be found in conjunction with the simple labour of the day. Religion, myths, anguish and wisdom — the soul of the people is represented in all its fullness.

'Black and red' the Pharaohs called their country: red like the incandescent sand, black like the fertile river deposits and the dense shade of the trees. Thus, from its birth Egypt was a contradiction, sterile and fruitful, open and closed. Here four worlds converged: the Sahara, Black Africa, the half European Mediterranean, and the Asiatic Near East. But a belt of water and desert encircled the oasis. Geography thus imposed on it a destiny out of the ordinary: the Egyptian civilization was to grow under the sign of the sun and the fertile Nile; it was to prove miraculously rich and essentially immobile.

Religious symbols are not invented. They 'grow', said Hertzfeld, rooted in a prehistoric humanity. The primitive inhabitants of the long valley were animists, worshipping the stars and the mysterious machinery of the days, nights and seasons which gave rhythm to their daily lives. In the second millennium BC the Hyksos poured across Western Asia, driven from the Eurasian steppes by the encroaching desert. They were shepherds seeking new pastures, and they brought with them a multitude of cults inherited from pre-history. They doubtless imposed some of these on the river dwellers of the Nile. At all events, they were to give Egypt two dynasties of Pharaohs, the horse and war-chariot, and, perhaps, an obscure god born of their wanderings: Set.

For four thousand years myths and symbols proliferated, growing far from their roots and continually absorbing new vigour and meaning. On night and light, on the land and the water of the Nile, an abstract world was built, moulded from good and evil, love and ideas, energetic life and a death peopled with shadows. As soon as Upper and Lower Egypt were united the Pharaohs proclaimed a theology which they imposed. The bird, again associated with the sun, took its place at the head of the pantheon. Nekhbet,

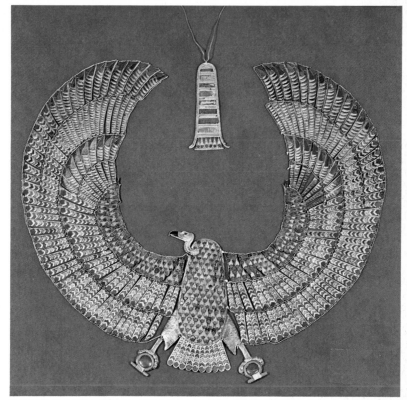

Nekha Bit, the vulture-goddess. Articulated pectoral in *cloisonné* gold, cornelian and glass.

or **Nekha Bit, the vulture-goddess**, ruled at first over the South assuring the protection of the king and adorning the head-dress of queens. Then she gradually became confused with Hathor, goddess of Love, and popular belief made her the protectress of all new life. Horus, the falcon with eyes of sun and moon, was originally the god of the heavenly spaces, before the unifying kings associated him with themselves. At the dawn of the first dynasty he was named 'protector of the king', sometimes symbolizing the Pharaoh himself. A combatant god, he watched over the strict observance of ritual and law. A god dispensing justice with a penetrating look, he saw the invisible through his *oujat* (painted) eye, a curious spot under his real eye. He was the sentinel at the gates of night, the watchful guard in the eternal shadows, before assuming his royal seat among the major gods; the theologians of Heliopolis, elaborating the 'Osirian cycle', made him the son of Osiris and Isis, the universal mother (every living being was a drop of her blood).

Horus the falcon, god of the Sun, surmounted by the disc of resurrection
Gold statue. Egyptian Museum of Antiquities.

Henceforth the corner-stone of the perfect triangle, he now represented the supreme Intelligence, child of the Cosmos and of Matter.

Pharaoh was the earthly branch of the cosmic tree, brother and messenger of the invisible gods, flesh of mysteries. He reigned alone over three thousand years of human lives, and he still reigns over the Cairo Museum, this land of the dead. The **sarcophagus of Tutankhamun**, the prize exhibit in this treasure-house of rareties, is made of gold-plated wood encrusted with glass paste — in metaphysical terms, plated with divine symbols and encrusted with the anxiety of the human spirit. Like the gods, the king wears a false beard. An animal's tail, fixed to his girdle, falls across the small of the back. In his hand he holds a sceptre with the head of Set, a demon in the form of a wild ass, the image of violence and night. Nekha Bit, the vulture-goddess of the South, guards his forehead next to the uraeus, which is both serpent of the Delta and the incandescent stare of the sun-father variously known as Re, Atum and Amun in different periods. Pharaoh is the son of his belly, fashioned by him, promised the most noble virtues and designated, even before his birth, 'to be in the palace'. He is represented at the moment of his coronation, climbing the steps of the throne and receiving the crowns of Upper and Lower Egypt in front of the princes and dignitaries. Henceforth, the light of the sky dwells in him. He is Horus incarnate. His father Osiris presents him to the celestial nobility and to the peoples of the Earth. Thoth the moon god in the form of an ibis, master of the scribes, writes his five names on the leaves of the sacred tree Ished. Then he is omniscient and perfect. His subjects venerate him and his enemies fear him. If his enemies rebel, he massacres them and offers to Re their heads bound in a sheaf. No-one will ever be able to find fault with his divine vigilance, and the people rejoices

Heads of defeated enemy chiefs, bound in a sheaf, offered to the god Re (XVIIIth dynasty, c. 1450 BC). Egyptian Museum of Antiquities.

because henceforth 'the happy times have arrived, a master has risen in all the lands, the flood rises high, the days are long, and the night has its precise hours'. Thus the reign of the god-man is absolute and incontestable, in accordance with the ritual books. According to the chronicles of the profane, however, his power was relative and beset with snares: no Pharaoh was ever free from intrigues, conspiracies and assassinations. After thirty years the Pharaoh celebrated Heb Sed ('the feast of the jubilee'). His divine power, weakened by the rugged life of earthly beings, is magically renewed, his

The sarcophagus of Tutankhamun (XVIIIth dynasty, c. 1350 BC). Egyptian Museum of Antiquities.

Thoth the ibis, god of Writing. Silver statue.

blood receives fresh life and he succeeds to his own throne. Then he dies, is identified with Osiris, god of the Dead, and beyond the night is reborn as the sun, ruling the skies with Re. On the earth of the living, a new master is consecrated so that chaos should not threaten and so that the balance between the two worlds should remain.

To conquer the shadows and to hold the void at a distance, such were the chief preoccupations of the ancient Egyptians. To soothe their fearful souls they therefore called on a host of gods who were given familiar forms. It is said that the invaders of dying Egypt — Persians, Greeks and Romans — were greatly amused when they found the relics of these gods: the majority of the two thousand divinities of the Egyptian pantheon were zoomorphic. There were few signs of humanity in this fantastic army: the venerated accomplices of the children of Re were bulls, cows, rams, crocodiles, cats, lions, beetles, ibises, falcons, vultures, serpents and fish. All were painted in a multitude of colours and carved with infinite respect,

piously mummified and invested with terrible powers, magical and preposterous.

It is supposed that the first inhabitants of Egypt were animal worshippers. They certainly made these animals the images of their hopes and fears. The tribal god of the primitive towns is known to have been embodied in some beast protected by taboos. Gradually the myth blossomed with its thousand branches, and from these primitive gods were born the great figures of the Egyptian theogonies. Thus **Thoth the ibis**, a lunar deity, was probably accorded a special veneration at Hermopolis before he came to reign over the creative word, writing, languages, mathematics and astronomy — in short, the intellect. The master of the scribes and the magicians, he was elevated to the rank of 'secretary of the gods', the guardian of the divine word. At Hermopolis, where there was a famous library, it was claimed that the god himself had deposited sacred rolls covered with illuminating signs in a secret crypt. Then the quest for the book of Thoth became symbolic of the mystical path leading to supreme knowledge. The Greeks finally assimilated the god with Hermes Trismegistos ('three times great'), master of all occult knowledge who was often invoked by alchemists even into the Middle Ages.

Anubis the jackal, god of Embalming and protector of the dead.
Egyptian Museum of Antiquities.

Lioness found in the tomb of Tutankhamun.
Wood covered with gold-leaf. Egyptian Museum of Antiquities.

Hathor, **the cow-goddess**, was less intellectual, less mysterious, and more solidly rooted in the vegetation of the earth. Between her horns, similar to the branches of the lyre, is the solar disc. She was made the 'golden goddess', mother of love, joy, the dance, music, the principle of all vigour, the nurse of the gods, of Pharaoh and of the mountain of the dead, the regent of the heavens and the living soul of trees. She too ruled at first over only a few capitals — which the Greeks named 'cities of Hermaphrodite' — until eventually countless sanctuaries were dedicated to her everywhere. As the myth spread, she was endowed with the virtues of Tefnut the lioness, and then became the protectress of a host of legendary figures and minor goddesses; seven Hathor fairies even appeared round cradles, impassively determining the destinies of the new-born. But despite this the cow-mother persists also and always as a deity in her primeval mould.

Presiding over the mysteries of the night was **Anubis the jackal**, god of embalming and protector of the dead. He was known as 'The one who has the bandages' and 'The one who is perched on his mountain'. It was said that this great funerary deity embalmed Osiris when he was killed by Set. In ancient times the conductor of the souls of the dead, he seems still to keep watch, imperishable, and, like one who is moved by nothing, to wait with open eye for our own worlds to crumble.

Over the land which the god Anubis haunted the scarab reigned, a sombre light, a sun assigned to the world of death. He was named

Kheprer and he engendered Khepri, god of the Rising Sun, and the verb **kheper**, which meant to assume bodily existence, both to be and to become. As protection against the pitiless eye of Horus scrutinizing the faults of the deceased on the scales of judgement, he was the golden shield fixed against the mummy's heart. He was the hope of rebirth. Kheprer thus represented a myth vaster than Egypt itself and one that possibly reached farther than its first inhabitants: the myth of the eternal return of wandering souls, like the sun being reborn every morning from its nocturnal ashes. Amulets were made of the god as talismans of happiness and hope. From earliest Antiquity the amulets were peddled throughout the Mediterranean basin, and they still are on the banks of the Nile. If a mischievous child holds out his hand and puts a green stone beetle in yours, think of the last survivor of the great Egyptian gods.

Apis was death, originally the sacred bull symbolizing fertility who became a funerary deity, and the fearsome crocodiles of Soleb were the gods of Water. All that remains of their burial places are giant sarcophagi, which bear witness to a metaphysical extravagance unparalleled in this world, and some touchingly simple words on fragile papyrus, like a letter to the future: 'I gave bread to the starving man, water to the thirsty, clothes to the naked. I have taken

Nefretiti, wife of Akhenaten (XVIIIth dynasty, c. 1370 BC). Egyptian Museum of Antiquities.

care of the ibises, falcons, cats and divine dogs; I have ritually buried them, anointed them with oils and swathed them with fabrics.' Mission accomplished, said the ancient Egyptian at the approach of death.

Yet the visitor needs only to be confronted by the representation of a human face as he passes along a gallery and immediately the animal deities are forgotten and the evidence is unavoidable: man is always more beautiful and more noble than his gods. In the room devoted to what the archaeologists call the 'Amarnan episode' are to be found **Akhenaten** and **Nefretiti**, who reigned over one of the great peaks of art and human adventure. In their time they were regarded as heretics for having invented monotheism. Regally splendid but disgraced as mortals who were too remarkable, they became the subject of legends.

Their history begins even before they came into the world. About the year 1400 BC Amenophis III married a Nubian commoner by the name of Tiyi. The priests were astounded and declared that a woman of the people could hold only a bastard to her breast. Only the sun Amun-Re, in the physical embodiment of the sovereign, and a princess of royal blood could give Egypt a future Pharaoh. When Tiyi gave birth to a son, the priests of Amun disputed his legitimacy. Then Amenophis III disputed the legitimacy of the priests, deciding that Aten, the life-giving ray of the sun and source of all energy, was no less a god than Amun-Re.

A new principle thus established, Amenophis IV, son of Tiyi, took the name Akhenaten and decreed the god Aten to be the unique, all powerful creator. Henceforth, all the other gods were mere idols. About 1370 he left Thebes and installed himself at Amarna, which was renamed Akhetaten ('the horizon of Aten'). There, with his wife Nefretiti, he served his great and solitary god, wrote hymns, inspired a new aesthetic system, sought for a new truth and, during a period of twenty years, created one of the

The Pharaoh Akhenaten (XVIIIth dynasty, c. 1370 BC).
Egyptian Museum of Antiquities.

Isis guarding the shrine of gilded wood containing the viscera of Tutankhamun. Egyptian Museum of Antiquities.

assembling the jigsaw puzzle, embalmed the gathered limbs and with the wind of her wings brought the dead Osiris back to life. Henceforth he lived eternally and symbolized resurrection for man. Isis gave him a son, Horus the falcon, whom she hid in the marshes of the Delta, at Shemmis. There she reared him, protecting him until he was strong enough to reduce Set to impotence and take vengeance for his father.

Since she was the perfect wife and mother, Isis became the protectress of love and of children. Since she was an infallible magician she knew the name of the supreme god, the name that must not be uttered, and reigned all powerful over the universe. In fact her glory was almost universal. Throughout the Roman world temples were dedicated to her, and festivals and mysteries celebrated in her honour. Then she sang, a light in the hearts of men: 'I am the mother of the whole of nature, mistress of all the elements, origin and principle of the centuries, supreme divinity and queen of the shades. It is I who govern entirely as I choose. The whole world worships me under many different forms, by different rites and under different names. Some call me Juno, some Bellona, some Hecate, others Rhamnusia, but the peoples of the two Ethiopias and the Egyptians, with the strength of their ancient knowledge, honour me with the cult which is truly mine and call me by my real name: Queen Isis.'

It is possible that the goddess was known in places remote from the Nile; some claim that the Celtic world and its Druids worshipped her. In fact, the cult of the serene Isis has traversed the centuries in many guises. In Paris, it is said, a temple was erected in her honour where the cathedral of Notre Dame now stands. Is she dead? Gérard de Nerval is doubtful: the breath of Isis has swelled the bosom of the lover since the time when 'the Pharaohs had statues made of themselves together with their queens, in very affectionate attitudes'. Thus in the

most luminous eras in the history of Egypt, leaving his kingdom to go to rack and ruin. Intoxicated with his god, he was unable to avoid earthly obstacles and fell without glory.

Then the gods, having been briefly eclipsed, again invaded the souls of men, led by the indestructible **Isis, the Great Mother,** her origins dating from remotest times. Like Hathor, she carries the sun between two horns. It is not known where her cult began. In the predynastic period her faithful seem already to have been established at Sebennytos, in the Delta. Her name means 'seat'; no doubt she was goddess of the royal throne before the theologians of Heliopolis made her the daughter of Geb (the Earth) and of Nut (the Sky).

After twenty-eight years of rule over Egypt, Osiris, her husband-brother, was murdered by Set the obscure who cut his victim into pieces and scattered his body to the four corners of the earth. Then Isis, as a good wife, aided by Nephtis and Thoth, wandered all over the world patiently re-

The Pharaoh Amenophis III and the queen Tiyi. Egyptian Museum of Antiqu

Nut, the goddess personifying the Celestial Vault. Papyrus (XIXth dynasty). Egyptian Museum of Antiquities.

statues of **Amenophis III** and **Tiyi**, the commoner mother of Akhenaten, Tiyi can be seen with her right arm held behind the king's back.

It has been said that the ancient Egyptians were fascinated by death. In fact, their petrified faces, the look in their eyes and their closed mouths testify to their stubborn love of life, their simple delight in love. These ancient people were so enamoured of light and warmth that they would try anything to find these things again beyond the ineluctable farewell of death. And so they set about constructing endless myths, gods, rituals, beliefs, placed lanterns on the prow of the funerary barge to deceive the night and erected religions as massive as the embattlements of a citadel. These religions evolved according to the whims of different dynasties, Pharaohs and eras, became obscure, labyrinthine and so complex that even today it is difficult to disentangle all the strands. In the inextricable undergrowth, however, four distinct roads are discernible which correspond to the four great peaks of ancient Egyptian civilization.

The first is known as the 'cosmogony of Heliopolis'. This is founded on the *Text of the Pyramids*, which says that one must believe in Atum, the first god, for he rose up one day from Nun, or chaos, built a hill on which the temple of Heliopolis was erected and became Re, the Sun.

The second is called the 'cosmogony of Memphis', dating from the beginning of the historic period, in the time of King Menes, who unified Egypt. It says that Ptah is the supreme god, the creator of order, cosmic, physical and moral. He is the vital force of Nun, father of Atum.

The third is the 'cosmogony of Hermopolis', so named because it was founded in that city. It declares that in the beginning eight gods

created the world and ruled over the Golden Age. Each has his female equivalent and all go in pairs; among them are Nun (Water) and Amon (Air). After a long period of peace they relinquished their earthly existence to go and live in an inferior world. But they continued to watch over mankind, regulating the floods of the Nile and the daily rising of the sun.

The fourth is known as the 'cosmogony of Thebes', the city which was the seat of government in the Middle Kingdom. It proclaims Amun to be the invisible creator of everything. In his person the various gods were merged. Thebes is the first city, built on the primordial hill born of Nun, the original ocean, and the other cities were built with Thebes as their model. Within its walls begins the history of the world.

How this world was seen is clarified by a fresco in the Cairo Museum: **the Goddess Nut** represents the Celestial Vault, her feet to the east, her arms to the west; along her sides the stars are depicted. Shu, with arms raised, personifies the luminous breath that animates earthly creatures. He holds Nut at a distance from Geb, her husband (the Earth). The nocturnal face of this world is death, the land of trials, through which the dead had to pass in order to return to life.

In the earliest times the rites of resurrection were reserved for the Pharaohs, the priests and dignitaries. Finally the people rebelled against this intolerable privilege, claimed the right to rebirth and obtained it. Henceforth at the burial of everyone the ceremony of the 'opening of the mouth' was practised, and all could undertake the great journey, embalmed in their tombs, provided with various funerary objects and with the *Book of the Dead* — the book of passwords needed on the roads to eternity.

First the deceased appeared before a tribunal composed of the

gods and the representatives of the forty-two *nomes* (provinces) of Egypt. They examined the conscience of the dead person, who recited his 'negative confession': he admitted to no sin and addressed himself in a familiar manner to his judges, like one who does not fear any verdict. Then rose Thoth the baboon, god of Wisdom and Reason. In the centre of the vast chamber was a pair of scales, between Anubis and Maat (Truth), who placed his emblem (an ostrich feather or his hieroglyph) on one pan; on the other pan was put the deceased's heart, the seat of intelligence and conscience. **Anubis observed the arm of the scales**, making sure that the deceased did not trick the assembly. Thoth noted the weight of the heart on his tablets. If it was as light as pure Truth, the assembly of the gods — the Great Ennead — returned a favourable verdict: the deceased then entered into eternal life, provided with a spouse and work. If not, without further ceremony he was thrown to the terrible Ammut, a monster with the body of a lion, hippopotamus and

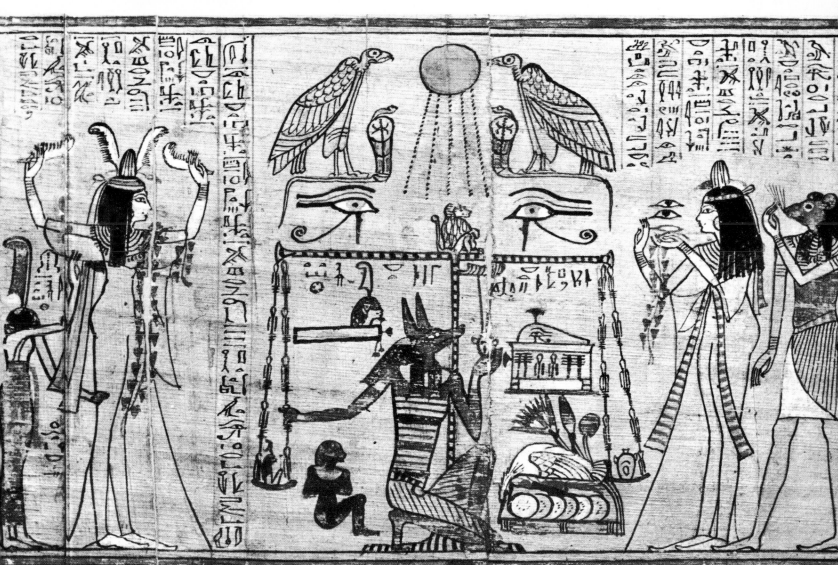

Anubis supervising the weighing of the deceased's heart. Papyrus. Eygptian Museum of Antiquities.

Late painting. Egyptian Museum of Antiquities.

they have a strange, artificial beauty which is imbued with a twilight quality. Man has banished the gods from these figures, the simple story has replaced the message and aestheticism has replaced the symbol. This art is by no means bad; it is merely moribund. It is no longer animated by any fundamental breath of life. Its *ka* is exhausted. During this time the Persians, Greeks and Romans in turn trampled over the 'red and black land', pillaging its civilization with violence and fascination. Their onslaughts caused the ancient religion to tremble but did not destroy it. During these so called 'decadent' centuries the cult of Isis reached its zenith. At Philae, Dendera, Esna and Edfu airy sun temples were built in her honour.

But death was close at hand. In AD 249 the name of a Pharaoh is for the last time engraved in hieroglyphs. The sun was falling, incandescent. It was given as many different names as the Eskimos have for the snow. It was believed to be immutable, but it was dying, and the great capitals, Heliopolis, Memphis and Thebes, were dying. Yet it is said that the end of any civilization is followed by a renaissance, and on the shore of the Mediterranean a new crucible was bubbling, Alexandria. Here a new vigour was born, the human spirit had the bright colour of new life. Greeks, Jews and Christians came together and quenched their thirst at the old spring, writing, speaking, thinking, searching feverishly for new spiritual paths, setting their souls in turmoil and attempting to build a bridge across the passage of time, between East and West.

Soon the Copts were to arrive. In the Cairo Museum their works are also to be found. Leaning against a wall, **a young Coptic woman** casts an anxious eye on the mingled waters of the centuries and gives a melancholy smile. She is very young — hardly more than a thousand years old. She was Isis in her previous lives. She knows that she will die and be reborn, but she does not

crocodile, who devoured him. Thereupon his *ka* evaporated, lost for ever in the inconceivable void.

The *ka* — a word untranslatable in our 'reasonable' languages. It signifies the vital force, the luminous power of the gods, the spark enclosed in every man. It also signified the reservoir of energy from which all life came and to which all life returned after death. The body was only the temporary vehicle of the *ka*. When the gods moulded the Pharaoh to come, they shaped his *ka*. When a man died he passed to his *ka*, the statue of his *ka* was placed in his tomb, and it was to his *ka* that the funeral rites were addressed. Where is the *ka* of ancient Egypt today? Perhaps here in this museum, where the visitor never has time in which to become accustomed to its countless faces. Yet it would be unseemly to leave this place without saluting the slow agony, the death and the final mutation of this civilization — the most venerable on earth.

In some rooms on the ground floor are the **works from the late Egyptian period**. They are two thousand years old, many of them dating from the Ptolemaic dynasties;

Portrait of Coptic woman.
Egyptian Museum of Antiquities.

know if she is eternal. Neither Anubis nor Thoth, the learned one, has told her. Now they are far behind her, and silent.

However, one must not try to travel in a straight line along the road of time. In Egypt the visitor should be prepared to get lost time and time again in the inextricable undergrowth of the centuries. He leaves the dead gods in the Museum, forgets them in the heaving throng of Cairo and then immediately finds them again reborn at the city-gates. The road leading up to **Giza** is lined with new modern blocks that already look old and with unexpected signs. Behind a Cleopatra Night Club and a Ramses Restaurant rise the too famous **Pyramids**, surrounded by a suburban district of cube shaped houses which are like insects launching an assault on eternity.

When you arrive, you will find any feelings of excitement somewhat dulled by what you see. The merchants are on the steps of the temple, peddling souvenirs, postcards, fake antiques, plastic beetles, badly painted plaster statuettes of Nefretiti, trumpery stuff of every sort; you will be confronted with garish *galabiehs*, toys, refreshment bars, water-melons, ices and multicoloured soda-waters. Hordes of tourists stroll about, American women lick ice-creams with their noses tilted towards the immutable, children in their Sunday best play among the camels and the asses, and guides laugh as they sell their skills and pose complaisantly against a background of sky, sand and ochre stone for photographers in gaudy Bermuda shorts.

You should leave this ridiculous and good-natured fair-ground as quickly as possible. You will not avoid the guide, and in any case he is necessary. Let him lead you, on a donkey or horse, towards the desert. As soon as you have crossed the frontier of silence, among the fawn coloured dunes, you will discover peace and the pure sun. All you will hear will be the quivering of your animal's nostrils, the buzzing of a solitary fly — time has been abolished. Now you can gaze upon the undefiled shapes of the most famous monuments in the world. They are what they were before millions of uninterested eyes, dawdling steps and graffiti devoured their awesome splendour. One day, three thousand four hundred years ago, on these same sands over which you tread, the young son of Tuthmosis II rode in pursuit of a gazelle. He paused to rest in the shadow of the Sphinx, which was buried up to the shoulders and already so ancient that the people of that time knew nothing of its origins. The young man fell asleep and had a dream. The legend says: 'In his dream he heard the voice of the god Harmakhis-Khepra-Re-Atum. At this time the sand rose to his face and the god begged to be delivered from this yoke which was stifling him. This the young prince did when, in his turn, he became Pharaoh.'

The Sphinx is today the most colossal statue in the world. Its lion's body with a human face adorned with the royal attributes measures fifty-seven metres long and twenty metres high. The

Giza and the Pyramids.

Arabs named it Abu el Hul ('father of terror'). Yet it poses no mortal questions, like its namesake of Greek Thebes, but reveals to whoever can read it the fundamental Answer, the secret of life. At least this is what certain esoteric thinkers believe. They claim that this colossus was erected in a distant age by the builders of a vanished civilization. In their opinion its presence induced the kings to erect their tombs here. It is true that statues resembling the Sphinx were found at Sumer, ancient Egypt's putative mother.

This is not enough to change the firm convictions of the archaeologists. The Sphinx, they say, was laid here during the first dynasties; its face is that of Chephren, brother of Cheops and builder of the second pyramid. When borings were made in its sides, no secret crypt or passage was found: the Sphinx concealed nothing. It remains for ever what the dynasties of the New Kingdom made it: Harmakhis, the god Horus of the Horizon, guardian of the western galleries of the Pyramids, along which the sun and the dead disappear into the distance.

On the evenings of *Son et Lumière*, its mouth delivers a noble text

The Sphinx at Giza.

by André Malraux. When the last projector is extinguished, the Sphinx smiles only for the stars.

Before you leave one last rite must be performed: you must cross the most sacred of thresholds and plunge into the heart of the Great Pyramid, built to the glory of Cheops, son of Snefru.

The narrow passage climbs steeply, and the heat is suffocating. The passage was made for a sarcophagus, not for someone standing upright whose *ka* is the prisoner of his body of flesh, muscles and bones. There is something oppressive about this place, something that can make the spirit dizzy. This tomb is four thousand six hundred years old. It is enormous: forty thousand square metres at the base, a hundred and forty seven metres high. To build it six million tons of limestone were quarried from the Mukattam hill. But the gigantic dimensions of the pyramid cannot in themselves account for the uneasiness felt by the visitor. More significant is the awareness of the spirits of a few men who vanished long ago, the sum of their knowledge, of their faith, of their metaphysical convictions and of their energy. Throughout the world there are mythical mountains which, it is said, unite land and sky. Cheops is one of them, it is not built of dreams, and here we are inside it. This is why our hearts beat too fast.

The four faces of the Great Pyramid are almost exactly oriented towards the four cardinal points. Traces have been found which indicate that the builder's original in-

tention was to provide an underground chamber at a very great depth. For reasons unknown this project, on the point of being realized, was abandoned. In the body of the pyramid a second chamber was then built which is reached by a gently sloping corridor. Once again the building work was left unfinished. Much higher up, at the end of a spacious passage known as the Great Gallery, a third funeral chamber was constructed. Its ceiling is made of nine blocks of granite each weighing four hundred tons. Above, five tiered compartments — the last covered with a pointed roof — avert any risk of the chamber crumbling under the weight of the great structure.

The Pharaoh's body was placed in the granite sarcophagus. Then access to the tomb was prevented by three great slabs arranged in the manner of a sliding door. Enormous blocks of granite obstructed the corridor. To allow the last workmen to leave a shaft was pierced leading from the upper extremity of the corridor to the first, underground chamber, the entrance to which was finally closed by a pile of rocks. How the great structure was erected is not known. One thing is certain, however: each

The stones of the Pyramids.

course of stones was laid starting from the centre and working outwards.

The Egyptians called their monument 'sea'. The word 'pyramid' is derived from the Greeks, in whose land it signified a pyramid-shaped cake. But why this strange structure was ever conceived remains a mystery. At first, in predynastic times, the dead were buried under rectangular heaps of sand. These mounds no doubt represented the hill of Atum who, according to the 'first cosmogony', emerged from the primordial waters at the beginning of the world. It is a powerful symbol, exalting life and challenging death. The steps of the earliest pyramids probably represented the stairway up which the deceased Pharaoh ascended to Osiris and eternal life. The pure geometry of the **Cheops** pyramid was also, perhaps, the image of the beneficent rays of Re, the star of the celestial summit, climbed by the king and down which, from time to time, he descended into the darkness of the tomb where the food offerings left by the priests awaited him.

The structure of the **Chephren** and **Mykerinos** pyramids is basically similar to that of Cheops. Around them stood a city of funerary temples, roadways and minor pyramids containing the bodies of dead queens. In ditches hollowed out of the living rock, at the foot of the Cheops pyramid, five solar boats were found: three were turned towards the east, two towards the south. Standing at the prow of one of them a dead Pharaoh perhaps symbolized the sun;

The Pyramids of Cheops, Chephren and Mykerinos at Giza.

perhaps he also sailed in the boat into the beyond, to rebirth. The first boat found, in 1950, has been rebuilt piece by piece and today lies stranded at the foot of the pyramid. It is a wonderful and awe-inspiring sight.

These too familiar monuments still conceal mysteries. A British scholar has suggested X-raying them in order to have done once and for all with the unfathomable. The esoteric school, for their part, claim already to have explained all obscurities. The meridian of the Cheops pyramid, they say, divides the Nile Delta into two exactly equal halves which proves that the ancient Egyptians possessed a very special know-ledge. The Great Pyramid, it is argued, reveals this knowledge to modern man: a message that is at the same time scientific, prophetic, philosophic and religious is inscribed in this book of stone. All one needs to be convinced of this is to be able to read into its structure. Nonsense, reply the archaeologists: there are no mysteries where science has applied its methods. No doubt they are right. Yet one cannot help thinking, as one looks up to their sunlit peaks, that here stand the masterpieces of a world which, quite rightly, put its highly developed science at the service of a profound mystery.

3

FROM CAIRO TO TELL EL AMARNA

Thirty-three kilometres from Cairo lies **Sakkara**. Three roads lead to this sun-baked place, for ever motionless in a world of endless movement. The first is the road that goes straight to Upper Egypt, following the course of the Nile. It is a 'good' road, as motorists say. It has a perfect surface and is of a banality that offers no surprises. The second runs along the desert, passing in a shimmering light between the hard pink sand and the pure blue of the sky — in a few days, as you approached Edfu, Luxor and Karnak, you would find yourself bathed in these same unavoidable colours almost to the point of intoxication. It is best to take the third road which, like the other two, starts from the Pyramids Road, a grey strip running straight between two hedges of modern blocks. Fifteen hundred metres before reaching Mena House, a white-walled luxury hotel ensconced in a peaceful garden at the foot of the Giza plateau, the road meets a canal. You should turn left and follow the canal.

Soon, as if by some trick of time, you enter the land of eternity. The day is green and gold, like every other day. Beside the foaming waters olive trees, coral trees and palm trees sway. You pass hamlets of tiny dried mud houses. Washing can be seen hanging across the terraces. Men go about their business, one on his ass, another pushing his slow buffaloes. Crouching on the river-bank a woman fills her round pitcher. She stops, watches you pass, calls to her child who is playing a few feet from her, and points at you. Cairo is still not far away, however — Cairo with its noise, its ramshackle buses, its shops, its hotels and its huge crowds. Here the *fellahs* (peasants) work and live. The peasant standing in the grass, beside the road, has watched without emotion the passage of Pharaohs, Greeks, Romans, Arabs, the passage of History itself over this land which resembles him so much — the same wrinkles, the same burnt skin — that one might think of him as the eternal Adam, fashioned from the earth. He watches, without realizing it, over a part of the memory of the world enclosed in the **Step Pyramid of Djoser**, in the tombs of the first dynasty princes and in the Serapeum. If he was not there, watching serenely, if his living humanity was not attached to these monuments by some invisible thread, their grandeur would doubtless be less moving.

Here once stood Memphis, the capital founded by King Menes. Now you see a plain,

Sakkara. The Step Pyramid of King Djoser (IIIrd dynasty)

Sakkara. Bas-relief on the mastaba of Ptahhotep.

fawn coloured, barren and splendid, and on this plain one of the most awe-inspiring cemeteries in the world. Twenty kings, their dignitaries and their peoples considered this desert the ideal place for their 'happy burial'. Under seven kilometres of dust and bare rock there still lie, perhaps for ever, innumerable relics, objects and dwellings of all periods rolled together like pebbles in a stream in the subterranean river-bed of time. Beneath the unbroken sky stand

mastabas (tombs composed of a chapel where the burial rite was performed and a vault into which the sarcophagus was taken) dating from the first dynasty, the Coptic monastery of St Jeremy and the Serapeum, a most strange place where a herd of mummified bulls was discovered in stone sarcophagi carved to their respective sizes and aligned along each side of a huge vaulted room deep in shadow.

One monument dominates this stupen-

dous anthology of Egyptian history: the Step Pyramid of King Djoser (p. 48). It is more ancient, less refined, more venerable and more solitary than its neighbours at Giza. It does not have the implacable grandeur of Cheops, but Cheops does not have its rugged beauty. It was built four thousand eight hundred years ago by Imhotep. This man was architect, writer, doctor, chancellor of the king and high priest of Re. His wisdom alone earned him a place among

life are a few guides and their asses, waiting at the end of the road in the wind and the dazzling sun. As soon as you enter the site, Imhotep's Step Pyramid is revealed. Like the legendary work of some demi-god, it is truly heroic. The pyramid is the culminating point of the whole necropolis, its heart of rock reaching to the sky. It is enclosed by a huge rectangle covering 150,000 square metres. The enclosure wall, with redans and bastions, reproduces in limestone the mud brick walls that surrounded fortified cities and royal palaces. From the enclosure wall begins a labyrinth of courts, rooms, roofs supported by beautiful columns, avenues, corridors and simulated doors (a way of saying without words that access to the heavens was forbidden to those who could not first rid themselves of the illusory appearances of this world).

In the centre of the labyrinth, at the end, as it were, of the initiatory journey, is the Step Pyramid of Djoser. This Pharaoh did not wish to wait for the inevitable resurrection, as his predecessors had done, under the same *mastaba* as his noble subjects. A *mastaba* was nevertheless built and traces of it can still be seen. But above it, for the glory of his master, Imhotep erected a monument of

six gigantic steps to a height of sixty-one metres. It was under the pyramid and not at its centre that the burial chambers, decorated with blue faience tiles and bas-reliefs, were found in deep crypts hollowed out of the living rock. The chambers contained the Pharaoh and his family.

The enormous tomb of Djoser is surrounded by a crowd of *mastabas*, intact memorials of the first three dynasties. The **mastaba of Ptahhotep** is one of the most beautiful. All are decorated with frescoes perpetuating the life that lay beyond the gates of night. Landscapes, straight trees, domestic animals, and fat plants swollen with juice express the pathetic hopes of these ancient human beings and their inordinate love of light. A stone peasant among the flowers leads three buffaloes held by a rope of twisted hemp. On your return from your journey to the centre of the earth you may well meet his twin-brother, driving his oxen and holding a similar rope in his fist. Together they express a fundamental truth: time does not pass, it reigns and respects whoever is unaware of it.

From the moving world to the motionless sky there was only a mirage to pass

the gods; the Egyptians honoured him as a god, and also the Greeks, for his renown travelled through the ages, and with justification: he was undoubtedly one of the greatest geniuses produced by the human race.

'I must have absolute silence to hear the voices of the ancestors', Champollion said one day. The silence he considered so necessary is here. Sakkara is not, like Giza, polluted by tourism. Almost the only signs of

Rural scene.

The Rhomboidal Pyramid.

The Pyramid of Meidum (IVth dynasty).

through. From the life of this world to the heights of death the Pharaoh Djoser climbed the six steps of the celestial staircase, a hundred times he came to taste the offerings placed in his tomb; at Sakkara he found the narrow gate through which he could cross, the needle's eye through which only innocent children and wise men pass. Beyond lay the land of mysteries.

Not far from the living, hard-working buffaloes is the temple of the dead bulls, the Serapeum, discovered by Mariette in 1851 and erected in honour of the powerful symbol of fertility. The bull Apis, resplendent and superb, traversed the whole of the ancient Egyptian civilization; he was born before it and survived it via Greece and Rome, before disappearing in the legends of the Western mythologies. In Egypt he was at an early stage confused with Ptah, the divine patron of Memphis, and then with Osiris, the god of resurrections. The death of the bull was a religious event, and spectacular ceremonies were celebrated in his honour. He was embalmed and, so that his journey into the life beyond might be accomplished painlessly, given a human burial place and showered with offerings. In exploring the underground galleries at Sakkara, Mariette uncovered twenty-four huge sarcophagi (the heaviest weighed sixty tons) hewn from granite and basalt. They contained the bull-gods, wrapped in bandages, who had embarked on a sumptuous phantom ship that would take them to eternity. They had lived happy lives. Even during the Ptolemaic dynasties they were assigned their place of glory (special spots on the white hide were used to designate a bull, the representation of which in other respects was distinctly banal). The bull, said the priests, was the incarnation of Apis and was therefore piously worshipped during his lifetime. His death, like that of the Pharaoh, was merely an eclipse, a brief change in the order of the world. The fields were searched for his new reincarnation, some fortunate calf was enthroned, feasts were ordered in his honour, and he was transferred to the sacred stable, where he spent a life of bliss amid a harem of cows.

On the floor of a room of the Serapeum which was walled in the year 30 of the reign of Ramesses was found the imprint of a sandal, left by the last man present in this place before access was finally prohibited. Thus, in this doubly sacred temple, even the transient became eternal. Further on from Sakkara lie three pyramids that present a sunlit enigma: at Dashur the Red Pyramid and the **Rhomboidal Pyramid**, and twenty-five kilometres to the south the **Pyramid of Meidum**. All three, erected at a most unusual angle of inclination, appear to have been built at the same period for the glory of Snefru, founder of the IVth dynasty and father of Cheops.

In the *mastabas*, in the shadow of the pyramids, lie the nobles, the viziers, the princes and princesses. They were not gods like the

Pharaohs. Their tombs, consequently, are not monuments to the celestial pantheon but speak of the earth, the lost mother. The men buried in them were in love with life and celebrated it with all their might before entering the next world. When they died their memories were of human faces and not of terrifying figures, of daily landscapes rather than heavenly spaces, of domestic animals rather than gods surrounded by stars. Thus, on the walls of the **mastaba of Tiy** (a dignitary of four thousand five hundred years ago) are to be found donkeys

Rural scene.

just like the one that awaits you at the entrance to the tomb, browsing in the sun on some yellow grass between two stones.

In ancient times, just as today, donkeys were loaded with weights heavy enough to break their spines, enlisted in the worst galleys, humble, patient and insulted at every opportunity. In this land where so many animals were gods, the donkey was never anything but a disgraced and abominated slave. The ancient Egyptians were loth to ride on it — anything was considered good enough for its back except the human posterior. The animal was

thought to be impure and maleficent. It was even suspected of concealing beneath its humble body the wickedness of Set 'the obscure'. In the latter centuries of the Egyptian civilization it was used only as a magic 'scapegoat': it was sacrificed to avert evil, and the scribes always showed it as fatally wounded, a knife planted in its spine. Those who travel by donkey today are only adding one more burden to its baggage. It is still despised but still tireless. Where is Apis the bull? 'Dead', says the donkey; 'I have never known glory, but I'm alive.' At Sakkara an anonymous artist portrayed this animal with tenderness, carefully shaping the curve of the ears and the gentle eye. The artist honoured it by giving it a place among the decorations of the walls of the tomb of Tiy, in an astonishing illustrated anthology of the society of Memphis in the Old Kingdom.

The beautiful frescoes depict the people: peasants pushing their ploughs, fishermen lifting their nets, shepherds submitting their flocks for the inspection of their masters, bookkeeper-scribes putting their reed-pens on the papyrus; the people play, dance, sing and hunt; a man is buried and they pray and weep. The profiles reveal the art of a fascinating draughtsman with a magical pencil. The lines are straight, austere and yet ironic: the scribes have the paunches of scribes, the dancers perform wild gestures, and the peasants have broad, confident faces, good-humoured and hirsute. Their life was tough, however, according to the writer who described it on papyrus in the Middle Kingdom: 'When the waters of the flood cover the ground, the *fellah* takes care of his tools; during the day he sharpens and grinds them, at night he makes ropes. Even his midday hour is occupied with agricultural tasks; like any warrior, he prepares his equipment before he goes into the fields. When the earth is dry he must spend several days pestering the shepherd to get him a team of oxen. At dawn he goes out to tend them

Sakkara. Bas-relief on the mastaba of Tiy.

and does not find them where they should be. For three days he splashes through the mire and finds them at last, but he has lost the harnesses, nibbled away by jackals. Off he goes, his loin-cloth in his hand, to seek another team of oxen. He spends his time continually growing cereals. The serpent, his enemy, destroys the grain he has sown, and the peasant does not see even the tiniest green shoot rising from the earth. Then he borrows some barley, but he must give his wife in exchange to the merchant, for he has nothing else. When the harvest comes, mice, birds, grasshoppers and cattle devour it. Thieves steal the crops from the threshing floor. The oxen die of exhaustion. Then the scribe comes to demand the tax on the harvest, and his Nubian servants give the *fellah* a beating and throw him, bound hand and foot, into his well.'

A sombre picture. It should be pointed out that this text was intended for the edification of an apprentice scribe. It was written to comfort the youth in his studies and to turn his thoughts away from the possible temptations of the bucolic life. It would therefore appear that some officials preferred the plough to the pen, which suggests that the condition of the peasantry cannot have been so terrible. Provided that the flood watered the land on the right day, that the Pharaoh and his vizir administered the country wisely, and that order reigned in all things, life would have gone on without any harsh shocks. It is known that the peasants possessed property, that they were not too ill-treated and that, in the event of a dispute, they could have recourse to the judicial authority, theoretically the incorruptible guardian of a precise and benevolent moral code. This code recommended that one should 'not lean against the small in favour of the great, and not use violence against men, either in the country or in the city, for they are born from the eyes of the sun'. Men are born equal, say the oldest texts of humanity. Alas, they add, men have invented inequality. From time immemorial the Golden Age has been a remote prospect.

Near the necropolis of Memphis is a

palm grove which surrounds a poor village, Mit Rahinah. Here are to be found a few vestiges of a temple of Ptah, an alabaster sphinx, an embalming table for the Apis bulls and, lying in the grass, a **broken statue of Ramesses II**, ruined and yet serene, asleep with the eyes wide open and facing into the sun. The bird of silence hovers over these ruins which were once Memphis, the first capital of Pharaonic Egypt and a city more vast than Thebes 'of the hundred gates'.

In the early historic period Menes the unifier founded Memphis at the exact dividing line between Lower and Upper Egypt. Here he built the White Wall fortress and assumed the double crown of the 'Two Lands'. Then, for seven centuries, Memphis reigned as absolute queen of the cities and townships. Even when the royal power moved to Thebes, the Pharaohs were eager to have residences here, and many of them chose to have their pyramids erected as near as possible to the old capital. About 2420 BC a new suburb was built near the pyramid of Pepi I, so that the remains of the divine Pharaoh should not remain alone among the sands. The suburb was called Mennefru, a name that soon referred to the whole city and which the Greeks pronounced 'Memphis'.

Memphis enjoyed a vigorous life of three thousand years. During these three thousand years, in the tutelary shadow of Ptah, creator of the world, master of all techniques and the legendary father of the great Imhotep, temples, chapels, palaces, dwellings and statues were erected, countless streets and roadways were laid, innumerable squares and courtyards built. Industries rose up and proliferated, weapons were made and warships constructed. All the boats of the Nile converged on its harbour. Herodotus relates that Tyrian merchants, Carian soldiers and barbarians of all sorts cruised there. Armies from Assyria, Ethiopia and Persia came to attack it, for no-one ruled over Egypt unless he held its heart, Memphis.

When the Greeks came they found the god Apis wholly to their liking and adopted him; they also discovered Imhotep and recognized in him the heroism of Asclepios (the Aesculapius of the Romans). Thus Memphis, having once been the peak of the Pharaonic world, remained a sacred place in the Graeco-Roman civilization. Unfailingly noble, it had known both the glories and the insults of time.

During the early centuries AD the ancient hill began to crumble, sapped by the waters of the Nile and beaten by human hurricanes. The final assault came from the Arabs, who reduced the city to a mirage. Where today are the enormous palace of King Menes, the house of Tiy, and the harp players under the porticoes whose melodies delighted everyone? Among the palm trees goats browse and the peasant passes on his donkey. Only the blade of grass is eternal.

At the twilight of the ancient Egyptian gods a new fire was lit

The palm grove at Memphis.

Memphis. The overturned colossus of Ramesses II.

Coptic monks.

produced before them. The splendour of the Pharaohs reduces them to silence. A few scattered monasteries and chapels discreetly concealed between pyramids and mosques cannot hope to hold the attention of the traveller dazzled by so many other sights. This is unfair. In Europe would not a fifteen hundred year old monastery be piously honoured, restored and visited? In Egypt there are monasteries as old as this which are condemned to remain in the dark shadow of the giants: the monastery of St Jeremy, for example, built in the fourth century and brought to the light of day in 1968, near the palm grove at Memphis. This building is worth a moment's attention, standing as it does at the threshold of the Christian era. For those interested in primitive Romanesque art, in purity and miraculous simplicity, another site deserves a slow detour: the very old Terenuthis, in an almond-shaped valley called the Wadi Natrun, to the west of the Giza plateau.

With Siwa, Khargeh-Dakhleh, Farafra and Baharieh, the Wadi Natrun belongs to the group of five great oases of Egypt distinguished by modern geographers. The ancient Egyptians counted seven oases in their country. The oases were of great importance, for food grew there in profusion, and myth also flowered: the oasis was not a 'gift of the Nile' but a mysterious present from the empty sky. It was called *ouhat* (cauldron) because it was humid and hollow on the burning sand. *Ouhat* became 'oasis', which in Antiquity was also called 'prairie of the ima-trees', the latter being high bushes often represented in the frescoes of tombs and temples and frequently mentioned in Pharaonic texts.

It seems to have been established that the majority of Egyptian oases — which, from earliest Antiquity, already had their date palms — were inhabited by prehistoric man. The oldest papyri mention their existence and always make a clear distinction between nomads and oasis dwellers, sedentary crop

on the old ashes, the great, solitary figure of Jesus Christ. The **Copts**, his witnesses on the banks of the Nile, elaborated new ways of life and thought, built temples and engendered an art. Today, however, their works have difficulty in making themselves felt against the mighty background of the noble antiquities of Egypt. They are overshadowed by the sheer profusion of the masterpieces

growers whose religion differed from that of the river dwellers of the Nile. Their god, a highly mysterious deity, was represented by a fetish in the form of a sceptre. It must be assumed that he possessed none of the vigour of Re, for he soon disappeared, the oases fell under the tutelage of the Pharaohs and were invaded by the new gods and temples. By the time of the Middle Kingdom their economic and cultural annexation was complete. Yet they remained somewhat marginal, isolated areas, like adopted daughters stubbornly surrounded by an alien scent. An ancient tale relates the adventures of a man with a fabulous gift for oratory who, from the Wadi Natrun as far as Heracleopolis, sold rare objects and exotic foodstuffs with a strange flavour. He is a fascinating figure, someone out of the ordinary — a man of the oasis.

Most of these islands in the ocean of sand were stockraising lands. But the ground was too fragile to support for long the weight of the herds, which disappeared for the greater part after demolishing the tender growths of the fields. The vine was also cultivated in the oases, but it, too, did not remain for long. It has reappeared more recently in the Wadi Natrun, which contained another substance essential in the time of the Pharaohs — natron, or native soda, without which the burial rites of ancient Egypt would not have been what they were, since this salt was indispensable for embalming the deceased. The corpse, from which the viscera had been removed, was soaked for seventy days in a bath of dry natron salt that completely dehydrated it. The period of seventy days was dictated not by any chemical necessity but by ritual. It corresponded with the astrological cycle of Sirius, at the distance separating death and resurrection. Thus, the prosperity of the Wadi Natrun lasted as long as embalming was practised. When the old religion vanished, the glass industry replaced that of salt. It was never as flourishing as the natron commerce

Wadi Natrun. The Coptic monastery of Deir es Suriyan.

which, right up to the dawn of Christianity, had attracted hordes of people of every sort — craftsmen, merchants, workmen and collectors of new myths.

In the third century AD the Wadi Natrun was invaded by monks, men of a mystical faith but by no means dreamers: the industrious valley enabled them to communicate with the world, and the frequent raids of the desert Bedouins were thwarted on the walls of Kom Abu Billu, their base. At first, in their pious fury, they demolished a temple of Hathor. Then they concentrated on making themselves an important centre of monachism, the doctrine of the ascetic hermits preached by Anthony and Paul of Thebes. At the beginning of the fourth century they changed the course of their philosophy and adopted the monastic principle; henceforth the golden rules were silence and the community life. Then monasteries began to appear all over the sands of the Wadi Natrun, and in the year 1000 there were more than fifty. Four have survived to the present day: Deir Amba Baramos, Deir Amba Bishoi, **Deir Abu Makar** (p. 61) and **Deir es Suriyan**. To

reach them you need to go by jeep. The tracks are vague and there is a danger of getting lost; but the guides know these monasteries and the roads that end abruptly at their gates.

The monasteries were built in the fourth century on the same model: an enclosure wall a dozen metres square surrounds several churches built one above the other, the monks' communal accommodation and the bell-tower, which was originally also a defensive keep. The peaceable men who live there, outside the world, know nothing of the efforts being deployed around their refuges, in the valley. Attempts are now being made to irrigate the arid land and to make wheat, oranges and vines grow on the rock and sand. Already there are some green fields — a hard-won victory. Twelve thousand people inhabit the Wadi Natrun, and one must hope that the winds of poverty will not be allowed to uproot them and take them away to the shanty towns of Cairo and Alexandria. Craftsmen, glassmakers and peasants (Allah helps them) struggle to survive, as do a few silent Christians (God be praised), under the

Wadi Natrun. Mural painting in the monastery of Deir Abu Makar.

incandescent eye of Re, the immutable.

Women are not allowed to stay at Deir es Suriyan ('the monastery of the Syrians'), and men cannot enter without the proper credentials (an authorization signed by the Coptic patriarch of Cairo is required). The other monasteries of the Wadi Natrun, though not as unsociable, are not inviting enough to draw the traveller constantly attracted by more accessible marvels. He therefore tends to go on his way, rebuffed in advance by these monks whose hearts would appear to be so firmly closed to the world. On the walls of their dwellings icons keep watch with eyes wide open.

These icons have the powerful expressions of men who refuse the dark slumber of the soul and also the defenceless anxiety of those who are afraid of succumbing to it. The artists who painted them were clearly influenced by the profane masters of the Fayum school who imposed Alexandrian art throughout the Mediterranean Basin. They were depicting ancient gods, and the new god, his apostles and his saints were represented in their likeness. The figures of Christ and of the Virgin in our Romanesque churches thus derive, by roundabout paths, from the last temples of Isis and Osiris, secretly speaking their language, the eternal language of the melancholy watchers, eyes open and mouths closed, at the threshold of perishable matter.

Thousands of papyri were also discovered in the monasteries of the Wadi Natrun. On these rolls were inscribed, at the beginning of the Christian era, translations of the Old Testament, of the Gospels and of the heretical texts of the Gnostics and Manichaeans. They are in the Coptic language: the writing is Greek and the words are borrowed from the popular dialects of ancient Egypt. Most of the manuscripts are no longer in the place where they were found. Scattered in museums, they inspire the artistic fancies of amateurs and the sacred passions of scholars. In 1852 a British

gentleman by the name of Tattam bought a thousand of them at Deir es Suriyan and presented them to the British Museum, which now owns the largest collection of papyri in the world.

In the tenth century the Arab conquest put a brutal end to the Coptic period. The monks were persecuted, and the last workshops deserted by the copyists were invaded

Wadi Natrun. The Coptic monastery of Deir Abu Makar

with dust. Their language suffered, lost its vigour and wilted like a tree planted too near a stronger one. Nowadays it serves only as a liturgical language, and barely one tenth of the Egyptian population still hears it in churches.

The Coptic language could, however, have had a glorious destiny. In the sixth century it was known as far as Nubia, where Christianity carried its crucifixes and banners, and in Ethiopia where the Church is still flourishing in the twentieth century. According to a tradition fifteen hundred years old, the Coptic patriarch of Alexandria still exercises a nominal authority over it. The patriarch is elected by the monks of the four monasteries of the Wadi Natrun. Let it be said, finally, that their retreats are less remote and forgotten than they might seem, and their silence more eloquent.

The Nile.

Bas-relief on the mastaba of Tiy.

north. It is the indisputable calendar: the first day is that of the first flood of the year. It is the horizontal tree of life rooted below the equator, in the strange landscape that surrounds the inland seas (the primordial waters?) which the British named Lake Albert and Lake Victoria.

It goes its way, from waterfalls to calm expanses, an impetuous torrent, a river as peaceful as the eye of Isis, through the Sudan, Nubia and Egypt to disappear into the Mediterranean six thousand five hundred kilometres from its source. It nourishes Egypt as a mother feeds her infant; without it there would be no arable land, no marshes, game or pools of fish, no grass or trees, no nocturnal dew, no clear water at the bottom of the wells, no life. Let it then be blessed among the gods, let it be loved, honoured and heaped with offerings, sang the Ancients. It has been thus celebrated unfailingly, since time began.

Today, as if it had grown with the passage of time, the Egyptians call it not *Ioteru* but *El Bahr* ('the sea'), and its song is sung on the **feluccas**: 'The wave is strong, captain, but the waters are not for ploughing and no foreigner will take them from us.' Thus the sailors reassure themselves, frightened by the thought that the life-giving bosom could be snatched from them. They have nothing to fear. On the slow moving waves of the Nile, peace seems more assured than anywhere else, profound and delicious. Wise travellers know this as they sail from Cairo to Aswan, on the 'Isis' or the 'Osiris', the sumptuous boats hired for their pleasure. They pass feluccas with sails gently swollen by the tepid wind, identical to the boats carved over four thousand years ago on the walls of the **mastaba of Tiy** at Sakkara, tiny villages of mud-brick houses, peasants, quietly going about their business under the palm trees. As they sail along they bathe in silent symphonies of ancient stones and forget that somewhere, far away, time is passing.

The language of these men who have let time pass them by has also travelled up the Nile, the inevitable path followed unceasingly by everything that lives, from source to sea and from sea to source. In this country all the streams of History, all explorations into the memory of the past, all roads lead to the Nile.

The Nile is in itself space, time and the gods. The Ancients named it *Ioteru* ('the river'), as if there was no other in the world, and sang on its banks: 'You are the unique, the one who creates himself from unknown essence. On the day when you come out of your cavern everyone is overjoyed.' Indeed, no happiness could be more justified: *Ioteru* was the absolute axis existing since the first dawn. It is the infallible serpent landmark: its body separates east and west, its tail is the south, its jaws the

The stele of Akhenaten. Egyptian Museum of Antiquities.

Not far from Cairo, beyond Sakkara, you will hear the first sweet sounds of the flute under the trees of the Fayum oasis, a region as beautiful as a cool evening after a boiling day. The Fayum province was once believed to be Canaan, the land of milk and honey which Yahweh promised to the Hebrews. All the evidence shows that it was the idyllic garden of ancient Egypt.

In fact it is a false oasis of one hundred and fifty square kilometres on the shores of Lake Karun. At one time this lake was vast, but the passage of time slowly dried it up, releasing fertile land. An arm of the Nile which the Copts called *Bahr Yussuf* ('the river of Joseph') joins it to the valley. Such is the map of the territory. According to legend this gigantic lake in the desert ('Blessed be it', says the storyteller) was a physical manifestation of the Cow of the Sky. Why, then, had she disguised herself as an ocean? To hide in her bosom her son, the sun with saurian jaws, who was fleeing from the rebellion of gods and men. All praise, therefore, in the words of the storyteller, to both the Cow and the rebellion which together caused these waters to flow for the perpetual prosperity of living creatures. In fact, the Egyptians built temples here to the glory of the crocodiles that infested the lake (this is why the Greeks called the place Crocodilopolis).

Eighteen hundred years before Christ, the Pharaoh Sesostris decided, in spite of his faultless piety, that it was unreasonable to leave as it then was a land too fertile to be abandoned to the gods. He therefore had dykes built which held back the swollen waters of the Nile. These waters swelled the lake, and from the lake canals were dug to irrigate the plain. Later the Ptolemies perfected the system by building a giant sluice-gate. When the Romans came they brazenly exploited this Eden and ruined it. Today over a million people inhabit the province of Fayum. In addition to vegetables and cereals, they grow fruits of such gorgeous

Tell el Amarna.

quality that they are exported to Europe.

After the Eden of Fayum both boat and train call at **Tell el Amarna**, so named by Bedouins who pitched camp here less than two hundred years ago. Three thousand four hundred years ago its glorious name was Akhetaten ('horizon of Aten'). Nefretiti, the 'lady of joy full of graces', lived in this city founded by Akhenaten for the dazzling but transient glory of his one and only god. Here, outside Egypt and time itself, his mystical dream seemed briefly a palpable reality. Below a curving mountain there are eleven **stelae** (marking the city's outer limits), remnants of temples, palaces, private dwellings and even of the village

where the building workers were accommodated. These are precious ruins, very rare in Egypt. In fact, they are the most important evidence of secular urban planning in the time of the Pharaohs. All that remains are some stumps of walls which the imagination longs to rebuild; but on the neighbouring mountain, on the faces of twenty-five royal tombs, there are some frescoes that show what life was once like here: people in the streets, women in terrace roofed houses, men in their bathrooms, children running to school, officials in their offices, workmen in arsenals, even policemen, and invisible but strangely present painters and sculptors.

Much has been said about their art. Some see the 'Amarnan episode' merely as a surrealistic nightmare. Others praise the brilliant genius of this moment of history outside History. All are agreed on one point: the reign of Akhenaten was marked, as if with the sun-god's red-hot branding iron, by some kind of revolution against the clumsy, rigid administrative system of the Pharaonic world. Perhaps this is what disturbs us most today, in the present troubled state of our world.

Along the Nile, to the south of Amarna, are Assiut, Abydos, Dendera and Luxor. From one town to another the *feluccas* with their lovely sails make their way along the

Paddle-boats on the Nile.

Barges on the Nile.

river, loaded with scrap-iron and wood, fruit and vegetables, and pottery the colour of the desert. They pass **paddle-boats** as beautiful as those of Louisiana in the old 'Westerns', taking well-to-do tourists to Aswan and calling out in greeting to the **river barges** which provide a shuttle service from one bank to the other, crammed with talkative, laughing peasants and all sorts of baggage, bicycles, goats and vegetables. The Nile could not go its way without the *feluccas*, nor could the people of the valley manage without *nokta*. The word *nokta* means a kind of desperate optimism, a sunny fatalism, a way of joking which is untranslatable under the grey skies of Europe. It signifies both the mood and the humour of the people of this region. To understand it one must first learn, with an open heart, to love a burst of ringing laughter from a melancholy face, a face caught in a reflection of the sun on the passing water.

At Assiut the boat enters Upper Egypt. Assiut is the largest cultural and commercial centre of Upper Egypt. It has a population of two hundred thousand, is provided with schools, technical colleges and a university attended in ever increasing numbers by students from Port Said. After Assiut you pass villages perched on hillocks along the banks, protected from the floods. A woman dressed in black veils her face and makes a sign with her hand. A child replies, lower down, at the prow of a green boat. Then you pass a Coptic church painted blue and a pink mosque standing erect amid a mass of brown houses.

In the Pharaonic period the villages were grouped into *sepets* or provinces, the distribution of which owed nothing to chance and everything to the intelligence of a centralizing power anxious to have complete control over the resources of each piece of its territory. The term *sepet* signified a stretch of land regularly intersected by canals and ditches. From the time of the unification of the two Egypts this system of land division, calculated in accordance with the requirements of agricultural yield, taxation and, above all, irrigation, was strictly applied to the country as a whole. The tribes haphazardly encamped on the fertile banks of the river were caught in the mesh of this net, and all that they retained of their ancient independence were their totems and their tribal signs, which made it possible to identify the boundaries of the new royal districts. In the Old Kingdom there were about thirty-nine, each administered by a delegate of the Pharaoh originally known as 'the one who digs the canals'.

Each *sepet* constituted an economic and fiscal entity, and the royal administration took a regular census of its wealth before assigning the greater part to itself. A census of the population was taken every two years, and the scribes had one sign to specify peasants of the male sex, another for women and another for expectant mothers. Wealth was subjected to a much more frequent scrutiny, and there are some tomb frescoes which give a precise idea of what these fiscal ceremonies involved. First came the commission of surveyors, whose task was to measure the arable lands,

Going down the Nile.

to draw up a list of their owners, whether individuals or institutions, and a list of those who worked the lands, to estimate future harvests and the probable tax yield. When the harvest was ripe there then appeared, with great pomp and ceremony, a jurist scribe, two scribes from the surveyors' office, a representative of the district administrator, a rope-holder and a rope-stretcher. They then fixed the amount of tax to be exacted and, according to the frescoes, a flogging awaited anyone liable for tax who was unable to pay. Cattle and poultry were carefully counted in similar fashion and regularly lost the proportion due to the king. It was clearly not the lesser part that he received.

Soon, however, the 'canal-diggers' and 'dispensers of fertility' who administered each province in the king's name were tempted to govern in their own right. They made themselves princes, and their sons succeeded them. The suzerain was thus often forced to fight his impudent vassals lured by the rewards of independence. Each period of disturbance was followed by a period in which the provinces were restored to order, with a variety of new measures that diminished the authority of the earlier laws and represented an attempt to break the chain of hereditary successions that were threatening the royal authority. Towards the end of the New Kingdom the number of *sepets* had increased from thirty-nine to forty-two, thus equalling the number of judges assisting Osiris at his tribunal. Neither their allocation nor their distribution corresponded any longer with the traditional list of the Old Kingdom.

In the temples, however, the ancient list continues to be used, for it was regarded as an image of the cosmic order of Egypt, its symbolic content speaking more clearly to the hearts of the wise than dry administrative precision.

When the Greeks arrived they thought the system so good that they kept it, contenting themselves with renaming the *sepet* the *nome* (the administrator of the *nome* became the 'nomarch') and making the burden of taxation even a little heavier.

This made little difference to the condition of the peasantry. The small private property which had existed under the Old Kingdom had long since vanished. Everything belonged to the king. Everything continued to belong to the state, whoever its master might be, up to the nineteenth century. Then large properties appeared and proliferated, always to the detriment of the peasants. In 1950 they occupied thirty-four per cent of Egyptian land. The property owners numbered twelve thousand, and there were over three millions who could not manage to feed their families by cultivating their little plots. In 1952 the first decision taken by Nasser and his team of revolutionary officers, all of peasant origin, was the agrarian reform which considerably relieved what had been a clear injustice.

As the boat passes village after village and through province after province, it is accompanied by birds.

4
FROM TELL EL AMARNA TO LUXOR

A ruined palace against a violent pink background, a solitary column on the threshold of the invisible (the temple is just beyond), a motionless landscape beheld with eyes half-closed behind a screen of shimmering light—as soon as the traveller enters Upper Egypt, everything draws him like the siren's song towards the dazzling and almost too peaceful mysteries of the past. The simple life is also to be found here. Hard-working *fellahs* lean over the tender green of the clover fields. Others walk, dragging their sandals, behind their camels loaded with sugar-cane. One must not forget these people. Just as the fruit is more delicious than its painted image, they are more necessary than art. Just as men are more precious than their gods, they are more fertile than the Nile. One must speak to them, greet them in their own language. Then, with heart beating as one leaves a royal tomb, one discovers that there is no higher expression of beauty than a tomato presented by a woman in a garden. 'May this journey be for you like a plate of cream', she says. You should reply: 'The sight of you is like the breeze of spring' and, finally, '*Saïda*' ('Goodbye') — such are the polite, unvarnished phrases of communication. Then you must leave, for time is pressing and the 'present-past' again lures the spirit.

Beside the road is a **pigeon-house** surrounded by a rustling of wings, an extravagant palace made of mud and pottery and rising to a point, like the palaces in fables. Then you come to Baliana, from where you go to Abydos, one of the most ancient of Egypt's ancient sites. Nearby, at This, the first dynasty in the history of Egypt was established five thousand years ago, the dynasty of the kings of the dawn, known as the Thinites. At Abydos they built necropolises and cenotaphs and had themselves buried. The glory of this place extended beyond their reign. Sethi I and Ramesses II erected temples here, still in a good state of preservation and very beautiful. But at Abydos the invisible is more famous than the tangible. Here, according to myth, the head of Osiris was buried when Set struck him down. Every year, in the sacred city, the mysteries of the god of resurrections were celebrated; the legend of Osiris, whose limbs had been scattered by the master of darkness, was mimed as piously as the Passion of Christ, the people's tears were not feigned when the hero fell under the blows of 'the obscure', and their joy was real when Horus the avenger pierced

A pigeon-house in the Nile Valley.

the assassin's heart. People came to see the performance from the four corners of Egypt, and countless pilgrims prayed to the husband of Isis that he would be merciful on the day of the weighing of souls.

From shadow to light: Abydos was a place of dark dreams, but at Dendera, the next city, the clashing cymbal of the sun vibrates in the pure sky, for here lies the temple of the 'lady of joy', Hathor the goddess.

Dendera gained a place in the history of archaeology by virtue of the late period of Egyptian civilization, but its origins are much more remote as is proved by some very precise texts. In the pre-dynastic period a temple was erected here in honour of Horus, a tribal divinity destined to join the ranks of the celestial élite. On this temple another was built in the time of Cheops and was dedicated to Ihi, god of Music, of whom Pepi I had a gold statue made in the IVth dynasty. From this time onwards, as the city walls were repeatedly breached, the builders restored them on each occasion, right up to the end of the ancient Egyptian civilization. The present day Dendera is the final result of this process of reconstruction; it is not older than the Ptolemies and the Romans.

Two sphinxes keep watch at the entrance to a labyrinth of galleries, chambers, terraces, crypts and chapels. Staircases lead up to the mysteries; the first floor of cult rooms is full of light, the last storey, near the sky, is all darkness. In her duality of depth and height, darkness and light, Hathor stands aloof from the vain meanings of words. The **twenty-four columns of the Great Hypostyle Hall** pay her homage: they are in the form of a sistrum, her first attribute. The sistra were a kind of musical rattle on which the face of the 'lady of joy' was inscribed. Twelve long and narrow rooms, very difficult of access, were hollowed out of the thickness of the walls. This sort of niche in the walls was not usually decorated, but these chambers are decorated, though precisely with what purpose is difficult to say. Some texts suggest that they were intended to be in imitation of secret underground sanctuaries where, in the darkness, the recumbent gods could drink from invisible springs and slowly feed themselves with the vigour necessary for rebirth.

The **frescoes of the temple of Hathor** show how each of the innumerable chapels was built for a particular practical purpose, some as libraries, others as laboratories, rooms of 'the renewal of forms' or 'chambers of the Nile', places for the birth of Isis, or Osirian sanctuaries. The chapel nearest to the upper terrace of the temple may have been an observatory for astronomy. It is decorated with a map of the sky inscribed with the decanates (ten degrees) and constellations of the zodiac. A cast was made of this important discovery and is now to be seen at Dendera (the original is in the Louvre Museum). A neighbouring chapel once witnessed

Dendera. Bas-relief on the temple of Hathor.

one of the principal episodes of the sumptuous festivals of the New Year, the 'union with the disc'. Throughout Egypt these festivals were celebrated with great pomp. At Dendera they were particularly splendid, as can be seen from the precise details of the temple's frescoes. They began two days before the New Year. First the clergy, the king's representative and the priest of Dendera, known as 'the musician', descended into the depths of the divine house. Following the 'mysterious corridor', they came to a shaft; through the 'house of flame' this shaft led them to a crypt where the statue of Hathor stood on a gold pedestal, protected by linen curtains. They broke the clay seal, pulled the bolt, uncovered the face, contemplated the form of its *ka* and sniffed at the earth. These rites accomplished, the goddess was carried on men's shoulders to the 'pure chapel' where she was anointed, perfumed, adorned with eight symbolical crowns and surrounded with offerings of jewellery and fabrics. Then, in the Great Courtyard, offerings were made of food, the vase of festival wine and the vases of milk, a pot of cream and the emblems of the two Egypts. During the night of the 'first Thout' the statue was hoisted onto the roof of the temple. Her face turned towards the East, she awaited the dawn, and when dawn

Dendera. The columns of the Hypostyle Hall of the temple of Hathor.

71

Karnak.
The columns of the
Hypostyle Hall of the
Great Temple of Amun.

came the rising sun caressed her, renewing her beneficent vigour. Then the musician shook his two sistra.

In the distance the people listened for the echoes of the sacred ceremony. When Hathor's music sounded, they began their celebrations to greet the New Year.

Today the last witness of these strange ceremonies is the somnolent sun, shining among the city walls now stripped of all their mystery. These stones are not immortal, for nothing in this life is immortal. Yet they assert their presence with the quiet power of a superhuman force. Beyond Dendera the traveller enters a semi-mythical city, almost terrifying in its colossal dimensions, Luxor-Karnak, the ancient Thebes.

Before confronting the giants you should wander along the Nile as the red sun sets in the blue grey of twilight. This landscape is one of the most beautiful in the world. You should also stroll through the lanes of the Arab village on market-day. The colourful crowds move among the low houses, the early-morning peasants have crossed the Nile on the ferry, loaded with poultry, vegetables, fruit, tanned hides, medicines and amulets. The children on donkeys, the women pushing goats, the powerful odour, the sunny colours, the shouts and the vehement harangues of the street vendors combine to present a vivid picture of bustling humanity. The traveller must pass through this beating heart before plunging into the silence of the city of the gods, three kilometres from Luxor. A horse-drawn carriage will take you there, by the road that runs along the Nile. Turning right at a crossroads where the French and American archaeological missions have their quarters, you take a short, sunken road to **Karnak**.

Immediately, one hesitates to utter a word; human speech cannot embrace the vastness of this sacred place. It is better first of all to hide behind the voice of a master: 'At Thebes', wrote Champollion, 'the ancient Egyptians used their imagination as

if they were men a hundred feet tall. No people, ancient or modern, has conceived the art of architecture on such a sublime scale.' An **avenue lined with ram-headed sphinxes** leads to the forest of walls, temples, statues and frescoes which relate two thousand years of Egyptian history, from the Middle Kingdom to the Roman invasion. To obtain a bird's-eye view of this ancient city covering some three hundred

Karnak. The avenue of rams leading to the Great Temple of Amun.

and fifty acres, one must make one's way to the top of the first pillar. Then, miraculously, chaos becomes order: the Court of the Ethiopians, the **Hypostyle Hall of the Great Temple of Amun** with its one hundred and thirty-four columns; beyond, the obelisk of Queen Hatshepsut, the granite sanctuary, the Festival Hall of Tuthmosis III, father of Amenophis II, and the east gateway. The Sacred Lake is to the right, and the vestiges of the tomb of Osiris, the temple of Khonsu, the temple of Opet and the temple of Mut in the distance, among the wild grass. To the north lie the Saite chapels and the temples of Ptah and Montu; to the west, near the avenue of ram-headed sphinxes, lies the quay of the sacred boat.

But whoever wanders in the silence of Karnak knows well that no mere inventory can ever account for the spiritual experience which this site offers. Here, in this gigantic place where frenzy is serene, where excess is calm and mystery sensual, one can only remain silent.

In ancient times an avenue of sphinxes led from Karnak to the **temple of Luxor**, in the southern suburb of Thebes. It is said that Amenophis III decorated the edifice with 'fine sandstone, on a pavement adorned with silver and laid on a bed of incense'. He also built the wonderful courtyard whose columns are like the budding lotus. Ramesses II built the forecourt and erected the colossal figures and two obelisks. At Luxor only one of the obelisks is now to be seen; the other is in Paris, on the Place de la Concorde. The temple was called 'harem of the south'; it was a sort of secondary residence of Amun, who here was identified with Min, the god with the straight phallus, symbol of fertility. Once a year the sun-god left Karnak for his sanctuary 'like the celestial horizon'. The Pharaoh presided in person over this journey, which was known as the 'festival of Opet'. Tutankhamun and Horemheb had the main episodes of this ceremony engraved on the great city wall of Luxor. This is what the carvings tell us.

At Karnak, before the sacred boat of Amun, the king made a ritual offering of flowers, fruits, poultry, meat, milk and wine, purified by water and incense. Then twenty-four priests dressed in loin-cloths carried the divine statues on their shoulders in procession, to the sound of music, hymns, fans and fly-swatters. When they reached the landing-stage they laid their precious burdens on the *feluccas*, and the Pharaoh took his place in the finest boat, next to Amun. On the river-bank the police circled the crowds, the people hailed the procession as it made its way upstream, with men hauling the boats to help the rowers, soldiers marched carrying flags, priestesses held the ritual instruments, the *menat* and the sistrum, in their hands, and musicians played, making a great din. The procession of boats moored at Luxor. A priest sang: 'You rise up in your perfection, Amun-Re, when you are in the Userhat boat.' The procession then carried the divine statues to the temple. On kiosks heaps of offerings were placed and consecrated by an officiating priest. Finally the god reached the heart of the temple where the profane was not allowed to remain. Here, for ten days, secret rituals were performed about which nothing is known. It is known, however,

Luxor. The mosque of Abu el Haggag.

Luxor

that during this time the people indulged in joyous celebrations. At the end of the ten days Amun was brought back to Karnak. For a year the festival was over.

Strangely enough, the festival has sur-vived to the present time. The **mosque of Abu el Haggag**, white and tiny, has made its nest among the ancient ruins. Once a year, on the day of the patron saint of Luxor, Sidi Abu is placed in a *felucca* and sails along the Nile, just as Amun once did. On the river-bank the people sing as they accom-pany the boat, among the horse-drawn carriages and cars. In the pure sky the sun-god is always present.

Theban necropolis. The colossus of Ramesses at the Ramesseum.

On the other bank of the Nile, in ancient Egypt, began the land of the dead. This place, the site of the Theban necropolis, is one of the most awe-inspiring in the world; a pilgrimage to the royal tombs buried in the barren rock stirs the heart, imposes the silence appropriate to sacred places, and compels the too mortal creatures that we are to meditate. At first, however, nothing on this left bank of the river is conducive to quiet thought. The landing-stage, a tiny construction of disjointed slats, is the meeting place for the villagers of the neighbour-

hood; at every hour of the day peasants gossip by the water, women dressed in black wait dreamily, a bundle of clothes on their heads, schoolchildren jostle one another and leap onto the ferry before it has moored. Life abounds, in the gold of the morning, splendid and simple.

The tourist in a hurry will no doubt have a hired car waiting. The wise traveller will probably prefer to hire a donkey at a low price, so that he can enjoy the journey at his leisure and relish the air. You pass branches of the river where the fishermen

lift baskets similar to those used five thousand years ago, women walking along the river, majestically carrying round jars on their heads, and you follow the bumpy road which runs straight across the green field. Buffaloes pass, slow-moving camels loaded with hay, and men covered with dust. Here, in the middle of a ploughed field, stand two monoliths of hard sandstone, reflecting the blue of the sky: the **colossi of Memnon**. In their familiar shadow a peasant pushes his plough, unaware of the motionless giants. This rich red soil churned

up by the ploughshare was once the site of the sanctuary of Amenophis III, and it is this Pharaoh whom the statues represent.

The two colossal statues are twenty metres high. One is of the king alone, seated on a huge throne; the other comprises three figures, with the queen-mother Mutemuia and the Pharaoh's wife Tiyi beside their master. On the throne were carved the symbols of the union of the 'Two Lands': two images of the Nile join the lotus and the papyrus, the emblems of Upper and Lower Egypt. When the Greeks and Romans discovered these colossi, they imagined in their stupefaction that they represented Memnon, son of Eos (Dawn). In the year AD 27 an earthquake split one of the statues as far as the waist; ever afterwards, each morning, the broken statue greeted the rising sun with a plaintive, monotonous chant. A wondrous mystery, said the Ancients, who believed that Memnon, killed at the battle of Troy, was groaning at dawn when Eos, his mother, appeared in the sky; heartbroken by her son's appeal she wept, and her tears fell as the morning dew. Nonsense, reply the scientists: the phenomenon is caused by the flaking of minute particles on the surface of hard sandstone, as the result of a sudden change of temperature. The reason of the scientist is always more correct; but the irrationality of the storyteller is always more beautiful, equalled only by that of the builders themselves, without whom there would be nothing but a ploughed field.

A few kilometres further on is another colossal statue, this one for ever silent. The **colossus of Ramesses**, hewn from pink granite, measured eighteen metres high and weighed a thousand tons. It now lies at the foot of the Ramesseum, its ancient sanctuary. Here, relates the old chronicle, was 'the castle of the millions of years of the Pharaoh Usimareh, the elect of Re, in the domain of Amun to the west of Thebes'. The Ramesseum is a magnificent ruin,

peaceful and surrounded by greenery. Here you can visit the ancient temple's storehouses, built of mud-brick and more solidly preserved than stone dwellings, and also the remains of the 'house of life' where the physicians worked, the scribes copied the *Book of the Dead* and instructed the living.

These places were no doubt inhabited at one time by sages refining their minds amid the buzzing of bees and the singing of birds, among the bushes and the flowers. Everything has remained except their transient lives. They knew it would be so. The mutilated face of Ramesses smiles to the shady trees and to the eternal grass swayed by a light breeze, but not to the living who too soon are dead.

From the Ramesseum a road leads to the land of immobility. It forgets the Nile and leaves behind the fields, the trees and the peasant people, losing life itself as it passes among sand and rock and finally ending abruptly against the western mountain of

Theban necropolis. The colossi of Memnon.

Mourners in front of the house of a dead person.

Gurnah. Mourners. Painting on the tomb of the vizir Ramoseh (c. 1370 BC).

Thebes. Here, in a rugged pink cliff roasted by the sun, lie the Tombs of the Kings. They dominate the Valley of Queens, Deir el Bahari where Hatshepsut had her mortuary temple erected, Gurnah, Dra Abu el Naga, Gurnet Murrai where the dead nobility were buried and Deir el Medineh where the builders of the necropolises — artists, craftsmen and workmen — arranged their own eternal resting places.

About 1500 BC, at the dawn of the New Kingdom, the Pharaohs, fearing that too conspicuous funerary palaces would soon be pillaged, decided that in the future their pyramids would be those built by the gods — the mountains — and that, in their quest for rebirth, they would have themselves buried in the heart of these mountains. Thus began the history of a place which centuries of sumptuous burials elevated to the rank of a sacred, semi-mythical land. There is nothing to be gained by trying to explore its magic, its beauty and its mysteries, for they are too profound. One must listen to the inexhaustible messages depicted on walls as the words of very distant and very strange wise men, and let oneself drift along in one's imagination as if in the solar boats of the ancient gods, seeking some improbable sign at the threshold of untranslatable knowledge.

Not far from the Ramesseum lies **Gurnah**, a tiny old village encircled by the barren mountain. For thousands of years its inhabitants have lived in the familiarity of the tombs, even to the point of having sometimes themselves chosen a troglodyte dwelling in the cliff: from a distance one never quite knows if a shadowy opening in the sunburnt rock-face is the entrance to a tomb or the home of a living person. The life of these mountain dwellers has hardly changed since Pharaonic times: the bread oven is like that used in ancient times, and so, too, are the food, the manner of ploughing a field, of threshing grain, of mourning the dead and humbly appealing for help to the master of human destinies whenever the harvest is bad or the tooth of the tax-collector too sharp. For countless centuries they have been poor. In former times they were too close to starvation to be able to live quietly so near to such impudent treasures, too overwhelmed by their condition to worry about being cursed for pillaging tombs — no sooner were the tombs occupied than they were plundered. Today these people can be seen digging on the archaeological sites, offering themselves as guides and carrying on a small trade in ancient objects, which are sometimes fake, sometimes genuine (a number of precious finds have been made among the dust and the broken stones).

On the square at Gurnah is the **tomb of the vizir Ramoseh**, who served Akhenaten. As one contemplates the paintings on the tomb, time seems to vanish, as at Sakkara. The life of this people who today enjoy the sun was depicted here more than three thousand years ago. One is struck by an overwhelming impression that the keen eye of the young guide has seen these **mourning women with quivering hair** and the funeral procession painted on the wall, in the half-light. The smiling man sitting in front of the tomb, between shadow and sun, seems to hear the chant written in the *Book of the Dead*: 'When the deceased depart for the great city of the dead, there is no pain in the livers of the relatives, nor in the servants and the friends who accompany them towards the beautiful West, behind the priests and the bare breasted mourning women, for all rejoice: O Amun! they are going to discover joy on the banks of the celestial Niles.' The melancholy woman rocking the sleepy baby at her breast, in the corner of a mud wall, seems to have sung the litany of the deceased's wife: 'Woe! Woe! I am your beloved sister. Why are you so far from me?' The priest in his ritual loin-cloth would reply: 'Joy is in the one who is now at rest. With the Osirian sign Djed he will be able to eat the food of Osiris.'

Winnowing grain near Luxor.

Gurnah. Scribes recording the harvest. Painting on the tomb of Menna (c. 1420 BC).

Mystery is a labyrinth all the more impenetrable because the step of the explorer is uncertain. The certitudes of the old Egyptians were by no means as sound as the gold of their tombs, they had doubts about their posthumous destinies and sometimes, confronted by the black ocean of death, gave way to the kind of ironic discouragement, the mood of desperate humour, which has always existed throughout the centuries and is nowadays known as *nokta*. The *Song of the Harpist* says:

'Generations disappear and go away,
others remain and this has always been so, ancestors,
gods existed once
and now rest in their pyramids.
Nobles and illustrious persons
are buried in their tombs,
they built houses which no longer exist.
What has become of them?
No-one comes from the world beyond to say how
    things are,
to say what he needs
to soothe our hearts until we ourselves approach
the place where they have gone.
This is why you must have a happy day
and never weary of doing so.
See, no-one has taken his possessions with him.
See, no-one has come back once he has gone.

'Have a happy day' — this is what they say in the villages, where they never know if the world will end tomorrow. Yet the **sakieh** turns endlessly, drawn by oxen and watched by children, like the eternal circuit of the sun; the precious water splashes the air and forms rainbows in the shimmering heat, streaming from the jars bound together like the ornament of a fertile goddess. The jars are baked in the communal oven in remote hamlets where the houses are barely more than topped walls: a single room is covered with a roof, humans and poultry sleep there jumbled together. Only the rich have a bed — a wooden bench. The occupants cook, eat and live in the closed courtyard.

Wandering along a dusty lane, you will spend a long time looking for something that could not have existed in such a place four thousand years ago. There is only one fountain of drinking water, in the centre of the village. The fountain is the evidence of a quiet victory, but one of supreme importance: it demonstrates that men have vanquished the gods. For a long time people quenched their thirst at the sacred river, whose 'fertilizing cream' was reputed to be beneficial in its effect, and many became so ill that they died (the waters of the Nile are infested with parasites). Today the terrible disease of bilharziosis, known as the eighth scourge of Egypt, is gradually diminishing, and the women go to fill their jugs at the clear fountain surrounded by children. The children are full of energy, but one must not say so to their mothers, for to speak aloud of the health of a son would be to risk arousing the jealousy of the demons and inviting bad luck. This is indeed a superstition of humble folk, the result of shattering poverty. People fear the envy of the fiends of hell just as they were once afraid of the cupidity of the great. In ancient times, however, when the yoke weighed too heavily on the peaceful peasants' backs, they erupted in violent anger. Famine was rife at a time when treasures

The *sakieh*.

Gurnah. The potter's oven.

and food were being piled up in the tombs. Pharaohs were building funerary cities of solid gold while the city of the living was crumbling into dust. Then, because no respect was being shown for elementary justice, the people revolted and killed, plundering the opulent tombs cluttered with their arrogant gold. One day, a woman accused of the crime of profanation said this to her judge: 'I found myself sitting and starving under the sycamores. I was sitting, starving.' She spat out the gods, stood up straight and swore to live her life outside the bounds of law and order. She was not alone. Others refused to commit themselves to the too heavy burden of service to the king, and so the Egyptians, who invented the soul, law and culture, also discovered the virtues of the strike.

Between the mortuary temples built on the western plain of Thebes and the rugged mountain range where the kings are buried their lies, in a narrow valley, a strange dead city called **Deir el Medineh**. To the west, in the sheer rock-face, tombs were hollowed out and decorated with prettily coloured pictures, their chapels crowned with tiny pyramids. They were never the burial places of kings, queens or princes. Workmen built them for their own eternity.

The clerks of the rule bound bureaucracy called them 'men of the necropolis team'. Themselves they described as 'servants in the place of Maat'. Foremen, quarrymen, carpenters, sculptors, painters and labourers worked together on a sacred site, building the tombs of the Pharaoh and his wives. Two hard-working teams replaced each

Deir el Medineh.

other every ten days. A royal scribe supervised their work, and their ultimate master was the vizir. With their wives and children these workmen lived at Deir el Medineh, a village built on the very site of their burial places. Much is known about their daily life. B. Bruyère, an archaeologist, spent thirty years exploring the places where they rested, their huts and domestic debris, deciphering the paintings and the chapels dedicated to their favourite gods, and translating the papyri of the supervising scribes, who were scrupulous and precise like the ideal journalist. Normally the people of Deir el Medineh did not suffer any oppression. The nobles held a high opinion of their merits and knew how to be generous with gold, praise and favours. In times of crisis, however, when things no longer went smoothly under the watchful eye of Re, strange things happened. A text preserved in the Turin Museum describes how something unparalleled occurred one day during the reign of Ramesses III.

The scribe relates: 'In the twenty-ninth year, on the tenth of the month of Meshir, five walls of the necropolis were smashed by teams of workmen who said: "We are hungry, for eighteen days have passed in this month." And they installed themselves behind the temple of Tuthmosis III. Then arrived the scribes from the prison, the two team leaders and the two district governors. Together they shouted to the workmen: "Return!" And they made solemn oaths, saying: "You will be paid, the king has given his word. Come and spend the night in the necropolis." '

'The officials had probably put the workmen's wages in their own vast pockets and were afraid that their victims would go to the vizir to complain. A night passed without bringing further news to anyone. By dawn the situation had become more bitter. The robbed men, confident of the rightness of their position, thundered: "Hunger and thirst have reduced us to this.

We have no clothes. We have no more oil, fish or green vegetables. Go tell that to the Pharaoh, our perfect lord. Go also to the vizir, our superior, and tell him to give us the means by which to live." Attempts were made to pacify them, and they were given the barley of the previous month, but they would not disarm. The vizir, whom it had been necessary to inform, arrived in person, making a firm but optimistic speech in which he promised a few vague favours; but for the time being, he explained, the situation was not favourable since the granaries were empty. Then work ceased and there were rumblings of revolt. It was necessary to negotiate without further delay. The strikers' first demand — not to die of hunger — was satisfied. They went back to work. Order had at last been restored.'

This is the story of the first strike in human history. The leaders, pious and gentle men, were capable of great masterpieces. Among them was Sennedjem, a scholarly and refined artist. On the walls of his tomb he painted on a yellow ground (he had no gold) scenes from the *Book of the Dead* and depicted his posthumous destiny with the luminous emotion of those who are sure of their art and their faith. The paintings show him kneeling before Osiris, his arms full of offerings, being led by Anubis who is also shown embalming him, and his mummy watched by Isis and Nephtys. Then he is seen opening the gates of the West, contemplating the gods of the sky and the underworld, sailing beside the sun, like the glorious Pharaoh. The funerary objects from his tomb are in the Cairo Museum with those of the Pharaohs. Re made men equal and blessed Sennedjem.

Beyond the tombs of the common people is the temple of Deir el Medineh, built in the Ptolemaic period, dedicated to Hathor and called the 'monastery of the city' by the monks who occupied it in the early years of Christianity. Farther on, at **Medinet Habu**, are the funerary temple of Ramesses III and a small sanctuary dedicated to the cult of Amun which stands, according to legend, on the very place where this major god was born. Places of worship abound at Medinet Habu; they are houses of gods, images of the world: their hard stone is the earthly plinth, their ceiling the starlit sky, and on their walls the sacred myths are painted. The plan of the 'castle of the millions of years' is unchanging. The faithful passed through its labyrinth, from light to shade, from the spoken word to the unutterable, from the profane to the sacred. There is not a single wall here which does not have a meaning, not a sign which does not lead from the land of men to the kingdom of the gods. These places are like the legendary gates opened, between dawn and night, onto the city of perpetual dreams.

Of all the funerary temples of Thebes the most beautiful and moving lies at **Deir el Bahari**, in the exact centre of the necropolis. Senenmut, the perfect architect, designed it and

Medinet Habu.

Deir el Medineh. The offering to Osiris. Painting on the tomb of Sennedjem.

Deir el Bahari. The temple of Hatshepsut.

had it built for the glory of the queen **Hatshepsut**, whose destiny was a strangely tormented one.

Hatshepsut was the daughter of Tuthmosis I. In the year 1490 BC, Tuthmosis II, her half-brother, took her as his wife and made her queen. Widowed, she proclaimed herself regent to the legitimate heir to the throne, Tuthmosis III, one of her husband's sons and her half-nephew. Tuthmosis III was never to be more than a sort of 'associate' Pharaoh, living in the august shadow of his aunt, a queen who exercised a firm grip on the helm of state and who liked to wear the royal ornaments and the false beard appropriate to the rulers who came after Re in precedence. In 1468 BC she died, whereupon her nephew's hatred exploded. The young man who had not known how to hold his own against the great lady during her lifetime had her statues smashed and her name erased from paintings and bas-reliefs. He could not — perhaps he dared not — demolish the temple of Deir el Bahari, hewn from the pink limestone of the mountain. Thus, despite his efforts, posterity was to remember Hatshepsut with gratitude, for her sacred dwelling is magnificent: a broad central ramp bordered with

Valley of Kings. The tomb of Tutankhamun.

decorated colonnades leads up to the successive terraces. There is no excess in this architecture, no indulgence in the colossal. It is miraculous harmony, pure music set amid broken rocks. Senenmut, the creator of this edifice, figures on a painting, behind a door of the royal temple. He did not wish to leave his queen after his death and so he had a tomb made for himself near her own. However, when Hatshepsut died, he was banished. It is not known how or where he died.

At the end of the necropolis is the **Valley of Kings** — the holy-of-holies. Three dynasties of Pharaohs rest here. Only one tomb escaped the plunderers, that of a minor prince called **Tutankhamun**, who attained glory among the sun-kings by bequeathing to the modern world the incorruptible mask of ancient beauty.

Howard Carter, who first brought the light of day to this famous tomb, discovered on the threshold of the sarcophagus chamber a clay tablet on which these words were written: 'Death will strike down with its wings whoever disturbs the rest of the Pharaoh.' In fact, many of the archaeologists among Carter's assistants died in a strange manner. Tutankhamun was therefore accused of posthumous murder. His curse, which was for a long time denied, caused a great stir. Philip Vadenberg put forward three theories: these untimely deaths may have been due to a virus capable of surviving for thousands of years in a mummy; or perhaps they were caused by a tiny poisonous worm that commonly infests caverns; some experts, on the other hand, say that the ancient Egyptians placed fatally radioactive objects in tombs.

No-one actually says so, but who knows if the ill-fated archaeologists were not killed, quite simply, by the powerful magic of ancient wizards? The resting places of the Egyptian kings reveal some old beliefs that may conceal an element of untranslatable knowledge. The mummy, surrounded by the figures of the deceased's relatives and attended by a host of servants in effigy (the *shawabtis*), is the refuge of the *ka*. The wall-paintings depict scenes from the *Book of the Dead*, the *Writing of the Hidden Room*, the *Book of Porches, Caverns, Day and Night*. They have magical associations: 'Nothing is', says the hieroglyph, 'before it has been uttered aloud.' Thus, the painted mystery becomes reality, the magic of illustration creates the truth. Empty myths? Perhaps, but fascinating none the less.

Near the tomb of Tutankhamun is the tomb of the **general Horemheb**, who put an end to Akhenaten's monotheist crisis. His final resting place was not completed. The paintings, interrupted in the course of their execution, reveal the pictorial techniques of the ancient artists. At the end of the journey to the land of the dead it is life that must be greeted, like the rebirth of the sun. Along the walls of the **tomb of Sennufer**, guardian of the garden of Amun in the time of Amenophis II, is painted a vine loaded with black grapes. Let him be named so that he may have life, since it is the Word that creates: at the rising of the sun. praised by Sennufer!

Valley of Kings. The tomb of Horemheb.

Valley of Nobles. The tomb of Sennufer.

5

FROM LUXOR TO ABU SIMBEL

In the distance are the temples, along the river people and gardens. This is the **Nile beyond Thebes**: it is as if the traveller is awakening after a dream. He has lived the fabulous journey through the labyrinth of the spirit and is now back in the world of simple human beings. A light wind swells the sails of the *feluccas* under the hot sun. Here the people do not worship Re, the thundering god; instead they love the father of the family. Here there is nothing to disturb the peaceful music of the days, and one dreams of finding eternity in this little Eden where the breeze speaks to the flower, to the leaf on the water and to the carefree tree. If it is true that climate moulds the souls of men, those who live in this region are certainly the gentlest and the calmest in the world.

The air of Upper Egypt is unique in its health-giving purity. It is free of pollution and humidity. The only rain it knows is the dew, and the only clouds tolerated in this perfect sky are the long white streaks left by aeroplanes flying to Aswan. Africa is near: the earth is red, the vegetation unusual, the sky a deep blue and the heat powerful. But the gilded green fields are still intersected by perfectly maintained canals, peopled by hard-working men, laughing, dusty children and women who hold themselves very erect as they walk along the paths carrying the work jars on their heads. Sixty per cent of the Egyptian sugar-cane harvest is cultivated in this region, but only 1.6 per cent of the country's gross agricultural product originates here. The temptation of single crop cultivation has proved a failure. This kind of intensive exploitation was exhausting the soil and barely providing the people with enough food. In 1952 the agrarian reformers decided that the necessary boost should be given to food crops, which alone could ensure the survival of the local populations. Today a great many *fellahs* work in co-operatives and they seem happy enough. You should make a point of stopping at one of them: after a feast of monuments, the sight of gourds, aubergines, fava beans and green peas is highly refreshing. A peasant, barefoot in a furrow of red soil, will proudly offer you some round, shining vegetable. You should accept it as a gift and you will remember, long afterwards, the touching smile which accompanied the presentation in a vegetable garden from some lost paradise.

However, one must not indulge in complacency and bless nature thoughtlessly. The flowing water was not provided by the gods, but was slowly and stubbornly conquered by men. Since the dawn of humanity these lands have been irrigated; the work was a daily task and the workers tireless. As early as the predynastic period they extended the benefits

The Nile beyond Thebes.

Esna. The columns of the Hypostyle Hall.

of natural inundation to the banks of the main course of the Nile. Basins were dug, surrounded by earth dykes and fed by canals: the basins of the upper river are filled by the simple force of gravity, canals directly joined to the Nile supply the downstream basins, and the last basins of the irrigation network take in any possible excess waters from the flood. The flooding lasts from August to October. Then the water draws back and alluvial mud is sown.

The highlands, which the flood could not reach, were at first irrigated simply with leather buckets. This was a hopeless task: four men striving to defeat the desert by watering half an acre each day. Then some ingenious person constructed an Archimedean screw — a wooden cylinder with a spiral screw propelled the water into the irrigation trench. Provided with this simple machinery, two workmen were able to achieve three times the yield previously obtained by four. The harsh desert was still scarcely receding. In the time of the New Kingdom the well with pumping-handle, called the *shaduf*, was invented. In the Ptolemaic period appeared the *sakieh*, the wheel of jars roped together and driven by donkeys or oxen — slaves' work. The *sakieh* is still in use everywhere on the banks of the Nile. It supplies the fields as far as possible, but it lacks the power of the modern mechanical pumps which this poor country cannot afford in sufficient quantities to tame the land of the sands.

The god-river was thus domesticated with the passage of time and served man faithfully. Thanks to it Esna, on the left bank of the Nile some sixty-five kilometres south of Luxor, is still the opulent agricultural city that it was in ancient times. Today it has more than twenty-five thousand inhabitants. At one time it was called Ta Sny. Within its walls reigned Khnum, the potter-ram who fashioned the human body in clay. The kings of the XVIIIth dynasty dedicated a temple to this god, as

Aswan.

did the Ptolemies and then the Romans, who built a superb **Hypostyle Hall** of twenty-four columns. Only the hall remains today, in the very centre of the modern town. At Edfu, near Esna, one of the largest Ptolemaic temples in Egypt was built and dedicated to Horus. It is still standing, and the innumerable signs inscribed on its walls have revealed everything about the rituals and myths prevalent here during the latter centuries of

Antiquity — yet another book that no wind will ever close.

Beyond Edfu is the first cataract of the Nile, the frontier-post between the void and life, chaos and order, the fierce desert and the oasis. Here the true Egypt begins. Here the god Hapi, lurking in his cave, spat out the fertile waves over the lands of the North. The river rises like the dawn and flows between its banks of hard sandstone,

Aswan.

their way into Egypt and the royal armies set off for war, heading south. Three quiet hamlets inhabited by a few Nubians remain on the island, which will never again be disturbed by the fevers peculiar to the frontier-town.

All the bustle of life is now to be found at the young Aswan. The modern town is very pleasant; its hotels are comfortable and its corniche road along the Nile offers some fine views. But it is in the old quarter that you should wander in search of the town's real life. Narrow, twisting lanes wind their way between squat grey walls. The doors are closed, the houses secret. As you come out of an alley the sun explodes in colours; a street stall, smelling of spice and pepper, is crammed with fruits and vegetables, dazzling the eye and the heart. Tall Nubians dressed in immaculate white *galabiehs* stroll about with a distant look in their eyes. The bazaar is crowded with people, black skins and brown, a wonderful medley of colours, mingling with the dogs and grey donkeys. In front of a Sudanese shop a little negro boy watches the carefree traveller with a smile and invites him to go into the shop, scented with pepper, a little dusty and slightly intoxicating. He sells gazelles' heads and stuffed crocodiles, gum, spices, embroideries, Nubian leather-goods and basketwork, ivory, ebony, shells and corals from the Red Sea, heavy stones. He sells the markets of Africa and the 'souks' of the East, the oasis, the savannah and the desert. One begins to dream. Where is Cairo now? Somewhere in the West, far away to the North. Here, as sun and shadow alternate, you catch in the eyes of people you pass glimpses of distant adventures, of naked childhoods lived between the caimans of the rivers and the warm flowers of the forests. Where is Egypt? It is here, immutable and silent.

On the right bank of the Nile, in a desolate, sun-scorched place, lie some ancient granite quarries which were worked in Pharaonic times. Here, thousands of workmen carved from the rock-face obelisks, colossal statues and giant sarcophagi. How many perished, driven mad by thirst, the relentless heat and the dust? Only the sun knows the answer. As if interrupted by some sudden catastrophe, their work was left unfinished. Almost detached from the mountain lies a crudely carved obelisk which would have measured forty-two metres in height. It is cracked, and perhaps this is why it never enjoyed the glory of belonging to a temple. What kind of madness dwelt in these men, that they should leave in the middle of the desert the fruit of so much hard labour?

Near Aswan is a lovely island, called Kitchener Island in memory of the British general who reconquered the Sudan after the Mahdi's rebellion. It has been converted into a botanical garden, a delightful place where hundreds of African and Asiatic species thrive in the privileged climate, a mass of fresh, multicoloured flowers perfumed with sweet scents and enhanced by the song of birds. There is another island whose beauty has been partly spoiled: **Philae,**

caressing the rocks, embracing the islands and feeding Aswan (p. 91).

At **Aswan** the East ends and Africa begins: the Tropic of Cancer passes through the town. The traveller should not come here in summer, for the heat is too overwhelming. But in winter the temperature is about twenty degrees Centigrade, the sky is perfect and the climate the most exquisite and the most wholesome in the world. Fifty thousand people live in this capital of Upper Egypt, which is flourishing under the impetus of tourism and new industry. In the time of the Pharaohs it was only an unimportant village. The chief town of the province was the island of Elephantine, 'the town at the heart of the wave' originally named Ieb ('the elephant'). It was a customs post and fortress built under the sign of the ram, the tutelary god whose mummy was found in a ruined necropolis. Through its gates the merchants from the Sudan and Nubia made

A stall in a street
in Aswan.

the island of Isis, which was half submerged by the construction of the first dam at the beginning of the twentieth century.

Two graceful pylons, long colonnades, closed rooms, a terrace and an immense court coloured with flowers are what remains of the temple of the Great Mother, Isis. It is surrounded by the airy and elegant Kiosk of Trajan and by some small sanctuaries dedicated to the goddess Hathor. In the time of Nectanebo, one of the last kings of Egypt, this was the favourite place for the cult of the faithful Isis; according to the old legend Osiris, her husband-brother, slept in the shade of a thicket on the neighbouring island of Biggeh, where no living being was allowed to set foot. At Philae, Isis patiently waited for the floods that were the signs of the god's cyclic re-births. She was worshipped with perfect constancy at a time when all the sacred places in Egypt had been abandoned. Even in the year AD 473 pilgrims came to her temple to pray and to engrave hymns on the walls. The First Mother, she was the last of the ancient deities to vanish.

When the first dam was built, Philae disappeared under the river. When the French novelist Pierre Loti passed here, he explored the hypostyle halls in a boat at night, cursing the progress that had devoured the sacred isle. For three months in the year the water receded and the muddy earth, almost as soon as it had reappeared, was covered with flowers, the temple rose up again in the sun, only to be submerged under the waves once more, like the shifting images of a dream. For a time it was feared that the builders of the High Dam would condemn the temple to perpetual oblivion. In fact, they have probably saved this stubborn masterpiece, and today every effort is being made to preserve it.

The **High Dam at Aswan** is the pride of modern Egypt. Before it, six dams had been built. The first five controlled the distribution of the Nile's waters and the sixth, constructed in 1902, contained them in the lake that covered Philae. Since 1956 it has supplied a hydro-electric plant which has made the introduction of new industries possible. Six kilometres to the south of the first dam, in a lunar landscape, the Nile has hollowed itself a bed thirteen hundred metres wide between two granite cliffs. Here stands the largest hydraulic structure in the world.

The High Dam is called Sadd el Ali and bars the river in a straight line. Behind it lies Lake Nasser, which is about five hundred kilometres in length and has a capacity of 150,000 million cubic metres; the lake controls the flow of the Nile even into Lower Egypt, abolishes drought, waters

Philae. The temple of Isis.

Aswan.
he construction
 the High Dam.

Nubia.
Children on the bank of the Nile.

An ancient village
in Nubia.

four harvests per year and can hold several floods of the Nile in reserve. This gigantic structure has tamed the sacred river, broken its sometimes tyrranical reign and transformed men's lives by increasing the production of crops already under irrigation. It has brought under cultivation more than a million acres of fields and gardens which would not have existed without it. Its power has been put at the service of the living: the hydro-electric station built on the Dam has made it possible to triple the consumption of energy, to develop stagnant industries and to create new factories.

The ecologist who ponders cautiously on the great achievements of modern science is not too enthusiastic in his praise, pointing out that the Nile is no longer flooding its banks. It was the floods that deposited the fertilizing silt on the soil of the 'black land'. But if there are no more floods, there will be no more alluvial deposits. Nature is no longer feeding the soil which is being exhausted by four harvests a year. It is now necessary to have recourse to chemical fertilizers to ensure that crops flourish. How long will it take for these fertilizers and the intensive harvesting to 'clean out' the Egyptian land? Only Allah knows. The engineer pays no heed to his critics: he has made it possible for millions of men

and women to live better lives and for the time being he does not wish to know any more about it.

Thirty-five thousand men worked day and night for years to build this giant; the price to be paid was the flooding of the land of Nubia. For thousands of years the Nubians lived on the fava beans and the sorghum which they cultivated on the bank of the Nile. Their language was African, sweet and melodious. Their houses were crenellated and decorated with birds and bunches of flowers which the children painted in whitewash on the fronts. It was a simple, naive and magnificent land, and it is no more. Near Kom-Ombo the Egyptian state has built for these poverty-stricken people thirty-three villages provided with social, cultural and commercial amenities. The houses are fine structures, large and solidly built. In this flat, sandy land these exiles are having difficulty in establishing roots. But the children make chalk drawings of flowers on the grey walls, as they did before. Perhaps the spirit is rising again in the Nubian peoples.

Under Lake Nasser lie secret traces of ancient buildings that no archaeologist will ever explore. Egypt could not sacrifice the lives of men to the memory of stones. There remained the still visible

Abu Simbel. The colossal statues on the front of the Great Temple.

masterpieces: they were unforgetable, and so it was decided to save them from the waters.

In 1959 UNESCO embarked on a campaign, roused the sympathies of forty-eight governments, collected funds from everywhere and mobilized all the Egyptologists in the world. Ten or so temples were moved and rebuilt where the lake could not reach them. The temple of Kertassi was pushed along the river-bank, as was the temple of Kalabsha, which was Roman. The temple of Amada is a fragile marvel of the XVIIIth dynasty; French engineers placed its eight hundred tons on hydraulic jacks, moved it two and a half kilometres and raised its height by sixty-five metres without a flake falling from its mural paintings. Wadi es Sebwah ('the valley of the lions') is an avenue of strange sphinxes (some have human faces, others the heads of sparrow-hawks) which led to the palace of Ramesses II. It is a remarkable fact that in the fifth century AD the Christians built a very 'ecumenical' chapel here where the Pharaoh is shown presenting flowers to St Peter and Christ figures side by side with Isis (see p. 104). The Valley of the Lions was hoisted to the top of the mountain which had towered above it. Other temples were dismantled and presented to the rescuing countries. There remained the mountain of **Abu Simbel**. Two hundred and ninety kilometres to the south of the High Dam, its **giant statues** contemplate Africa, apparently immutable. There are four of them, they measure twenty-seven metres high and are carved out of the rock-face. They guard two temples which Ramesses had built for his own glory and that of his wife, Nefertari. The mass of stone had to be cut up like a cake and rebuilt at the top of the mountain, sixty-five metres above its original level.

This fantastic task was accomplished with an astonishingly scrupulous concern for detail. It began in 1965. By 1966 the colossal statues and the two temples had been reduced to one thousand and thirty-five blocks weighing twenty to thirty tons, numbered and wrapped in straw. The blocks were then hoisted to the top of the mountain, where the new site was prepared. The lake would wash the stones and the sun would shine on them just as they had done previously. On 26 January 1966 President Nasser, the new Ramesses, laid the first stone of the rescued Great Temple. In 1969 the work was finished.

Tourists flock to Abu Simbel, which they had never heard about until its existence was threatened. So that these stones should not perish forty-eight countries — whom the fate of the living Nubians had never disturbed — provided funds and worked together with passionate enthusiasm. The Dam was responsible for this astounding miracle. A few inhuman aesthetes had cursed the Dam, but it is probably inhabited by some god or other — only a god could have made men's minds as fertile as the land and inspired such solidarity.

Abu Simbel. The dismantling of one of the pillars of the vestibule of the Great Temple.

Abu Simbel. Detail of the front of the Great Temple.

There is now no road leading to the temples of Abu Simbel. From Aswan, to reach this ancient site which has been hoisted out of time and ordinary geography, you must go by aeroplane or motor-boat. Voracious tourists claim that they can 'do' the sanctuaries of Ramesses II in a single day — one might as well content oneself with looking at postcards. Those who do not wish to skim over the surface of dreams allow the crowds to pass and wait for silence. At Abu Simbel you will find a comfortable hotel where you can stay. Here, in the high cliff rising above a wide curve of the Nile, before the High Dam levelled everything, a god-man wished to leave the imprint of his seal of power, to honour his gods and to express his love of a woman called Nefertari. He created a gigantic and tender monument.

At first you see only the **colossal statues** (p. 98). The plinth of the temple is the mountain itself, the sanctuary is its child. The four statues represent the king. They guard the temple on the south side, two on each side of the entrance. Leaning against the mountainside, they seem to illustrate the most beautiful myth on earth: the first man, barely fashioned, strives to free himself from the belly of chaos. His legs are heavy, well proportioned to the body but not quite detached from the earth and not quite free of the rock-face. The torso is less restricted: already in this sandstone a heart beats. Twenty metres higher up, the face is quite independent of the rock. It is sceptical, melancholy, lucid, conscious of the present, distant, smiling, foreign, benevolent, familiar, indifferent, divine, it is terrifyingly human — everything a human face can be when its owner knows the world beyond the earthly road. One might say that it touches the sky and discovers that it is empty.

Round the colossal figures of Ramesses, like frightened children, are his mother, his wife, his daughters and his son, huddled against his knees. Above the entrance the falcon-headed solar god, Re-Harkahte, stands erect. At the top of the **facade of the Great Temple**, dog-headed creatures engraved in a frieze hold out their arms to the sky. To each side are two chapels. One, hollowed out of rock, was 'the house of the birth of the rising sun'. As you enter the temple the floor rises gently towards a series of rooms, at first enormous (forty metres long), then gradually smaller. The sanctuary, at the highest and darkest point of the sacred place, is barely seven metres wide. Here are to be found the gods Ptah, Amun, Harkahte and Ramesses himself, deified. To the north a **smaller temple** is dedicated to the goddess Hathor and was built in honour of the queen **Nefertari**. The figure of the queen appears on the walls, slender, grave and beautiful, sometimes in the likeness of Hathor, sometimes accompanied by the two ladies of tenderness: Hathor, joyous love, and Isis, fertile fidelity. On the **facade** she never appears without two figures of her king.

Along the chain of relay posts that were situated on the navigable course of the Nile as far as the Sudan, these very high temples were undoubtedly, from the time of their construction, of great strategic and symbolical importance. The traveller, the mercenary and the

Abu Simbel. The front of the temple of Nefertari.

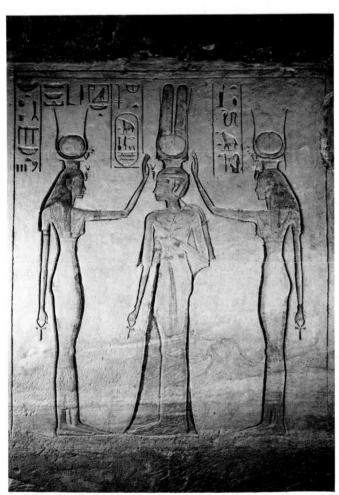

Abu Simbel. Bas-relief on the temple of Nefertari.

colonized Nubian leaving the 'black land' passed in the shadow of the temple of Ramesses the great, the powerful, the invincible, whose authority must not be forgotten. Whoever entered Egypt, travelling downstream, first saw the temple of Nefertari which spoke of love, maternal happiness and the homeland rediscovered after a long absence.

The archaeologists responsible for the Herculean task of moving the temples were not able to ensure that Abu Simbel remained the lighthouse at the gateway of the Egyptian Nile, but they have respected the basic intention of the ancient builders. Less than one kilometre in distance and at a height sixty-five metres greater than their original site, the temples have not changed their orientation. Every year, on 20 October and 15 February, the sun penetrates to the heart of the sanctuary and salutes Ramesses. Men have achieved the prodigious feat of changing their lives without disturbing the gods.

6

FROM SUEZ TO ALEXANDRIA

Underwater in the Red Sea.

As one moves away from the Nile, Egypt becomes a land the colour of glowing embers. To the west, the Libyan Desert merges into the blue foam of the Mediterranean. To the east, the Arabian or Eastern Desert extends as far as the transparent shore of the Red Sea, with its green waves and sun-scorched roads.

To reach the Red Sea one must go from Keneh, in Upper Egypt, to Kosseir, a small port with white houses two hundred and four kilometres away. The track is now mac-adamized, but the journey is by no means easy. The heat is intense and can drive the traveller to distraction, until he feels to be part of a mirage. One is allowed to drive only in company with several other cars, and official permits, provisions and petrol for at least three hundred kilometres are necessary. The track is cut out of the fawn coloured sand, the flint, quartz and alabaster. It is beautiful as the pitiless dream of a surrealist of genius is beautiful. From Kosseir one reaches Suez by the road that runs along the shore. The **marine fauna and flora of the Red Sea** are the richest and most dazzling in the world. One must be careful, however, about where one bathes, for sharks are known to infest the calm, transparent water, the bunches of flower-fish, the coral reefs and turquoise seaweed. Those who fear the hidden snares in these shifting paradises should stay at Hurghada where, protected from the sharks' teeth, they can enjoy the amenities of a marine biology station, an aquarium, a museum of fishes, a fishing club and, of course, the splendid sea.

One can, of course, go straight from Cairo to Suez by one hundred and forty kilometres of excellent road. In this important economic and strategic region everyone knows that there is a canal, and that along this canal History with a capital H has passed. To replace the canal of Pharaonic times which, up to the eighth century AD, linked Suez with the Nile and thereby with the Mediterranean, a few enthusiasts, among them Leibniz, had dreamed in the century of Louis XIV of

The Suez Canal.

cutting through the isthmus. This idea, taken up again at the time of Bonaparte's Egyptian expedition, was slowly to make headway until finally Ferdinand de Lesseps brought it to fruition. On 17 November 1869 the Empress Eugénie inaugurated the **Suez Canal**: henceforth, there was direct communication between the Red Sea and the Mediterranean.

The cost of this famous canal, in money and in human lives, was colossal, but it was to repay a hundredfold all the tears and gold expended on it. In the present century Turks, British, Germans, Arabs, Israelis and French have left their blood on its banks.

In 1956, when Nasser nationalized the Canal, it was providing fifty per cent of Egypt's revenues. Around 1830 some Utopians in the mould of Saint-Simon had hoped to make such a canal a means of union between peoples. Many died, broken by their obsession with brotherly love. Since then, this strange corner of the world has always had a troubled history.

Suez, Port Said and Ismailia are all names which speak loud and clear of the difficulties of the present time. The Sinai peninsula is another area of fierce dispute. Other places in the 'black and red land' bear witness to Christianity, like the **mural painting at Wadi es Sebwah**, in Upper Egypt, on which **St Peter** is seen receiving royal homage. But the Sinai has the spirit of the Bible written into its mountain masses. This Biblical association imposes on one a spiritual vagrancy — it irresistibly raises the spirit not out of the world, but onto the world's highest immaterial peaks. Some lands are vast, others are high: from the Pharaonic Nile to the Christian desert, Egypt indubitably belongs to the former.

The Sinai Desert is mountainous; its highest peaks rise to three thousand metres and are not unaccustomed to snow. It is an inhospitable region; through its mountains of pink sandstone veined with green the beds of the abrupt torrents rarely carry the clear water as far as the rugged valleys, which resemble the chaotic mass of some distant planet. Oases are few and far between, and grass is almost totally absent. Five thousand ghost-like, wandering Bedouins inhabit this wretched land, like the misanthropic anchorites who, in the third century AD, came here to live, to meditate and to die, defying the world.

Among the bare rocks there is, however, one peaceful and awe-inspiring place called Gebel Mussa. Here, according to tradition, lies the Mount Sinai where Moses received the tablets of the Law and encountered the Burning Bush. By the year AD 300 monasteries had sprung up around the

Wadi es Sebwah. Painting representing St Peter.

The monastery of St Catherine in the Sinai Desert.

sacred place. In the sixth century Justinian had the **fortified monastery of St Catherine** built, which served as a refuge for the clergy persecuted by the Arab conquerors, withstood all the storms of the centuries and has succeeded in preserving its treasures to the present day. Anyone wishing to visit it must leave Suez at dawn, cross the Canal by ferry, pass the tiny oasis of Ayun Mussa ('the springs of Moses') and climb a rough track leading into the desert. The venerable edifice is ensconced at an altitude of 1530 metres in the pink rockface of Gebel Mussa, surrounded by cypresses, olive trees, gardens and vines. This spot is the colour of prayer, for ever serene. A few monks still inhabit the maze of stone

and wood buildings, terraces, staircases and courtyards. They have in their possession four thousand icons (Byzantine, Greek, Coptic and Russian) and a library of Babel-like proportions containing three thousand manuscripts (Greek, Syriac, Arabic, Slav, Georgian, Coptic and Armenian), codices, liturgical texts of all periods and a fourth century parchment Bible. This is indeed a little paradise, among the books and works of art, the flowers and the orchards. The breeze whispers in the wise man's ear that no-one should be told about it.

There is another place blessed by peaceful gods where the biblical venturers never came to pitch their tents. It is not a sacred place, but is very much alive. It is called

Girl at the oasis of Siwa.

Siwa, an oasis planted in the heart of the Libyan Desert, in Western Egypt. Siwa is a remote spot, like the dream of an adventurous child.

To reach Siwa you must set off on a fine morning from Mersa Matruh, on the Mediterranean coast, and travel for ten hours across the sands. The road is partly asphalted. A few wells and reservoirs are to be found here and there, but they are often dry. In any case, they must only be used in case of extreme urgency. It is therefore necessary for cars to travel in groups, and they must have petrol and water for six hundred kilometres (to cover the journey there and back). Along the route it is possible that your 'caravan' may not meet a living soul. A few graceful gazelles may leap in fright in front of the strange, wobbling animal that you are driving. If so, you must not follow them or hunt them — fortunately this is prohibited.

Having left at dawn, you will arrive at twilight, thirsty with the sand, worn out with fatigue and the heat, and sated with the dazzling desert. At Siwa you will find a lovely **palm-grove**, the clear blue water of a fountain and the quiet voices of human beings. Here you can rest and rejoice in the peacefulness of this place. An

underground sheet of water emerges at Siwa in countless springs whose waters are soft or sulphurous, cool or warm, and it also enables two hundred thousand date palms and forty thousand olive trees to flourish. Six thousand people live here, partly Berber, partly Bedouin, partly Sudanese and partly Arab, and their faces express a very simple happiness. They press their olives, barter their dates for some sacks of essential goods and grow masses of flowers which they put on the fronts of their houses, give to their children and their guests, and place on their tables on special occasions. They are dreamers, a hospitable people proud to count among their ancestors a wife of the Pharaoh Cheops. They have not always been so peaceful. In the seventeenth century an obscure quarrel over a survey divided the seven clans of the oasis. Those of the eastern area, whose ancestors were priests of Amun, engaged in battle with those of the west. The fighting was ferocious and left an enduring bitterness — not long ago every family in the east still had his special enemy in the west, and not a year passed without the feud being ritually honoured in battle.

Fortunately, Siwa's past has known more glorious times. There was once a temple of Amun here (Alexander came to consult its oracles) and also a sublime fountain whose wonderful benefits were praised by Herodotus. In prehistoric times there was a village of tiny, rickety houses made of sun-dried mud, like toy huts built by children. It still exists, but is now almost totally abandoned. Nowadays the people of Siwa observe an important law concerning water rights, a law elaborated according to a highly complex system of common law. Nothing, in fact, is simple, for everything here depends on the goodwill of the springs. Custom ordains that the sexes be rigorously separated from the age of puberty. The women live as recluses, and at night the men leave the village. Until quite recently marriages between boys were recognized in civil law — everything was, and still is, ordered so that children should not proliferate. The fountains, the trees and the fields demand that this should be so, for they could not feed too large a population.

Today, however, tradition is dying. Egypt has need of the men whom the oasis does not want. The past is now the new enemy. The hairstyle with the ritual thirty-seven plaits that young girls used to wear is forbidden in school. The sweet old language of Siwa is also prohibited and cannot be spoken publicly without a fine. The invisible springs that used to nourish the spirit of these people will soon have dried up. Certainly, some were bitter springs, but others were good. No matter, new wonders are already being invented — a cinema has just been opened in the village.

Beyond Siwa lies Libya, to the south the desert and to the north the Mediterranean. As you head north, idleness and a gentle breeze await you patiently. This stretch of coast, where you can acquire a golden skin and fall asleep with your feet in the water, has been

Cotton picking in the Nile Delta.

the scene of battle and death. At Damietta soldiers slaughtered one another at the time of the Crusades, and at El Alamein armies tore one another to pieces at the height of the Second World War. A few rusty ruins remain, and some vast fields of crosses. After a feast of bathing, Alexandria, **the Nile Delta** and the plain of papyrus plants offer more fruitful pleasures. In this flat land the climate is fresh and humid, rain sometimes falls from the cloudy sky, the river loses itself among the marshes, the fields grow green well beyond its banks and Upper Egypt is forgotten. In predynastic

times towns were founded on the islands of sand that emerged from the marshland and enjoyed an enviable prosperity: in the rich soil fruits and vegetables grew in abundance, fish swarmed in the waters and game among the papyrus plants. It is not at all surprising that the first monarchs of the 'black land' should have so eagerly desired to unite this flourishing kingdom with that of the South, more noble but less prosperous. They knew that Egypt deprived of the Delta would never have been anything but a tree without foliage.

In the last millennium of Antiquity

northern Egypt was a royal province, as is indicated by the large necropolis of Tanis and the city of the Libyan Pharaohs, the last rulers of Egypt before the Ptolemies. Nowadays it is immensely productive; towns are numerous and well-populated, industry is thriving and agriculture is being practised on an intensive scale. In addition to citrus fruits and wheat, cotton is grown. In fact, cotton is Egypt's basic source of wealth and is of exceptional quality. It was certainly not so in the nineteenth century. At that time the *fellahs* wore themselves out on poor fields which could not produce enough to give them a decent living. Then Louis Jumel, the French agricultural expert, came and discovered a variety of cotton of unique quality and sturdiness. He gave it his own name: 'jumel' is today the best cotton in the world. Egypt naturally sells it at a high price and feeds itself on this trade, which brings in one hundred and fifty million pounds per year, a very satisfactory figure if one considers that total exports amount to two hundred and thirty-eight million pounds.

The money is hard won, for cotton growing is not a painless process. It demands daily attention and an abundant supply of manpower which crude machinery cannot aid. The cotton must be planted, weeded, thinned out, cleaned by hand and watered every fortnight. Each branch must be watched carefully and protected against the voracious worms that are quite capable of destroying everything. The **cotton harvest** comes in July when the ripe cotton plant blossoms in fragile, pale yellow flowers. Then the whole village goes into the fields: the children cut the crop, the women provide a rhythmic background by singing songs as drowsy as the sun itself, and the men go to the factories where the cotton blossom is taken almost as soon as it is cut. There they gin the cotton and pack it, thereby earning Egypt's daily bread.

Of course, as everywhere else, the old traditions are dying. Anyone who has never lived the hard life of these people has no right to regret their passing. A vigorous peasant tradition remains in the villages of the Delta, which is the last refuge of popular cotton growing. An Egyptian intellectual by the name of Wissa Wassef founded a **weaving co-operative at El Harranieh**, near Cairo. Here children weave some wonderful tapestries without using a pattern, reviving some soul-stirring images that one had thought buried for ever in Antiquity. Wissa Wassef thought that these workshops of spontaneous art should be multiplied so that the important pleasures of inventing, imagining and living should not die. He would be most welcome in the Delta. Let it be hoped that the simple art of the peasants will be given new life, that its gestures, its colours and its happiness will be reborn, and then one will be able to dream of the possibility of a golden age in this rich and populous country where men, in love with their country, speak readily of its daily wonders as they laugh into the sun.

The traveller finally comes to **Alexandria**, the city where a whole world died, where a thousand doorways opened, where everything was said and where nothing

The weaving workshop at El Harranieh.

was ever assured. It is twenty-three centuries old, and its founder was Alexander the Great, the conqueror conquered. It was Arab, Greek, Christian and Muslim, African and Western. Between the last fires of the ancient world and the dawn of the new era miraculously it knew no night.

Today it has a population of two millions and is the second largest city in Egypt. Its well-to-do modern blocks, its promenade, its sumptuous hotels and its palaces disguise it vaguely to look like some old watering-spa, under the sun and the palm-trees. Before the last war it was the favourite meeting place of a carefree high society: Egyptians, French, British, Greeks, Jews, Syrians, polyglots and decadents turned it into a sort of Babel-on-Sea, with a delicious and bizarre charm that always remained unspoilt. From this time which died before it could grow old, Alexandria inherited the most fantastic of flea-markets where everything can be found — all sorts of trifles, strange souvenirs of dismal gilt, shabby bric-a-brac, fake antiquities and also some genuine master-pieces. A few dark basements are still cluttered with statues, Graeco-Roman vases, relics and ancient coins. No-one seeks out such things now, except for shrewd tradesmen with long fingers and an appetite for the new money.

Since the revolution beautiful Alexandria has slumbered like a rather weary old aristocratic lady. It is no longer alone. Industrial districts have proliferated between Lake Mariut and the sea — the new life is here, feverish and rough. *Feluccas* with heavy bellies are constantly mooring at the banks of the canal, coming and going from the Nile to the harbour laden with round fruits, thin men, boxes and scrap-iron, amid the noise of shouting and singing. Nearly all Egypt's exports pass through the harbour. Along the quays the traveller, like a tight-rope walker between two worlds, can find himself fascinated by the bustle of the transit traffic, losing all awareness of himself among the stale smells of rusty cargoes and the wailing of sirens. In the distance, in the tepid mist, the tall cranes of the naval dockyards shimmer. Farther along still lie

Alexandria. The sea front.

some superb deserted **beaches** where the sea knows nothing of the labours of sailors.

In this city which finds itself in a state of unstable equilibrium between two continents and three religions, one must go back a moment in time. When Alexander conquered Egypt he founded the city and made it the most Greek of cities outside Greece. The conqueror placed the Ptolemies on the throne. Wise heirs, the Ptolemies respected scrupulously the customs and beliefs of their subjects, stimulated the arts and built palaces and temples almost worthy of Egypt's glorious times. Ptolemy II presented the new capital with the Pharos (Lighthouse). This is what the geographer Strabo says at the beginning of the Christian era: 'The tip of the little island of Pharos is merely a rock beaten by the waves on all sides. On this rock stands a white marble tower of several storeys, a wonderfully beautiful structure which is called the Pharos.' Its fame crossed the seas. In its light was built the museum, in the very centre of the city, and dedicated to the Muses. Here there were lecture-halls, a dining-room, a zoological park, astronomy laboratories and a library — the famous library of one million volumes which was possibly, at the beginning of the Christian era, the largest and most precious treasure in the world. Here, for a time, lay the centre of the human planet. Scholars, poets, mystical philosophers, sceptical prophets, those in search of knowledge and also the curious — in short, all the earth's spiritual travellers — met under its colonnades, discussed, dreamed, wrote, meditated and questioned the stars, creating a whole new world of ideas. The benevolent sovereign paid generously for their work. Alexandria, the capital of the Mind, reigned over the universe of the Word. As Athens declined, it assumed her place, welcoming the Greek light. As Rome grew, it scorned her power: it was to Alexandria's museum, and not to the Roman Senate, that Euclid came to speak.

Time passed, destroying everything. Of this astounding springtime of the spirit nothing now remains. The Pharos was one of the Seven Wonders of the World, but it is now submerged beneath the sea. The Greek city, white and harmonious, lies inaccessible under the Arab city and the modern blocks. All that is known is that it was built like a chessboard. The Ptolemies were twilight monarchs. No effort could prevent night from falling on an old Egypt at the end of its strength, destroyed by the erosion of the heart and by the invading vigour of the new peoples assembled on its frontiers. In the year 30 BC Octavius defeated Antony at the battle of Actium. Cleopatra committed suicide, and the child Caesarion was murdered. The 'black and red land' was no more than a Roman province. Then began Alexandria's inexorable decline. The city was still the capital, with a population of five hundred thousand including Greeks, Egyptians and Jews. In AD 117 Hadrian visited it, undertook some large-scale building works,

erected a few magnificent dwellings and went to philosophize in the museum, where people armed with ideas and words still tried to hold back the final catastrophe. Plotinus and Porphyrius lit the fires of Neo-Platonism. Philo sought God, admitted his existence and declared that Intelligence alone could reach his high dwelling-place.

Intelligence was indeed the last remaining bastion of an Alexandria which still thought itself powerful, unaware that a new era had just been born outside its walls and not hearing the din of foreign armour on the horizon. The sages of the museum sensed that no-one would be able to master the times that were coming, but they continued, imperturbable, to construct ideas like new houses. They awaited death like true men — with their eyes open.

Death finally came. It took a long time to close, one by one, the doors of buildings and the mouths of men, to efface the memory of porticoes and of human speech. When the Arabs pitched their tents in the suburbs of the city, four thousand palaces

The beach near Alexandria.

Alexandria.
The Roman theatre.

Alexandria. Pompey's Pillar.

in tombs of children, youths and young women, and never in any other place. In the museum one sees Pharaonic art making the transition to Christianity and one is astounded, as if by the sudden blossoming of a rare flower — for a brief moment time is magically vanquished.

In the sun lie the **ruins of the Roman theatre** with its tiers of white marble and columns carved from Aswan granite. To-

The market at Alexandria.

were still standing, a thousand gardens still flowering. When Bonaparte swept in, a population of seven thousand was slumbering in the torpor of a little fishing port with no future. Here and there, among the **sunlit markets**, the mosques and fountains, a few relics of the past remain, like the last fragments of a remote language that has taken the road to oblivion.

The Greco-Roman Museum contains some splendid specimens of Ptolemaic and Greek statuary. These statues stand side by side with some luxurious Latin works which are heavy, crude and devoid of soul. Two hundred years before Christ an anonymous artist carved in white marble a magnificent woman's head with the curly hair appearing from under a shawl. An enormous statue hewn from a monolith of porphyry has not revealed the identity of its model; some experts think that it represents the Emperor Diocletian, while others consider it to be a Christ Pantocrator. Next to it is a collection of genuine *tanagras* or statuettes of coloured terracotta discovered

wards the south west quarter of the city are the catacombs of Kom el Shugafa, built on three levels around the second century AD. The style of this vast funerary structure hovers awkwardly between Egypt and Rome. Near it stands **Pompey's Pillar**, thirty metres high, which is surrounded by Pharaonic debris and sphinxes borrowed from the ancient Serapeum and from the museum that stood nearby. Its builders clearly did not know to which civilization to devote their energies and so they chose their own time, uneasily situated between two eras, a time of silence and not of masterpieces.

In the wavering capital, during the first centuries of the Roman period, there were

The sun setting on Alexandria.

some people who were too intelligent. To revenge himself for their sarcasm, Caracalla had all the young men of the city herded into the stadium, ordered their massacre and dissolved the academies. The time of pillage and murder had come. Alexandria suffered war and fire, and its buildings were razed to the ground. Amid the dust and the flames, however, ideas continued to advance, apparently invincible and strangely brilliant. As Plotinus and Philo concentrated their minds on monotheism, a school of Christian theologians, the *Didaskaleion*, was established. Clement of Alexandria and Origen were its great teachers. Their intelligence stubbornly resisted storms and destruction, ensured the triumph of Christianity and built the Church of Alexandria on firm foundations. The Church spoke loud and clear, engaged in all the theological controversies that came its way and asserted its vigorous independence in the debates of the Councils.

The Church of Alexandria was tolerant and did not despise the great achievement of the old pagan faith. Undoubtedly, in spite of all catastrophes, the Alexandrians were still too clever. Within two hundred years the Catholic emperors were to bring them to heel. The Serapeum was savagely demolished, the famous library was burnt down — an infamous crime — the temples were closed and the too tolerant philosophers persecuted (the lady Hypatia was stoned to death in 415). On the ruins of the Caesareum built by Cleopatra the cathedral was erected. Several centuries later, events of a decisive gravity were to take place, and the cruelty of the Roman Church's representatives pushed the Alexandrian Church into an alliance with the Arab world. If the quarrel had been less ferocious, Alexandria would probably have chosen the West as an ally and the destiny of the Middle East would have followed a different course.

Then the Gnostics arrived in the disrupted city. This was to be the period of the great murders. They claimed to have received the foundations of their doctrine from some mythical ancestors and from Jesus Christ himself. In fact they were Alexandrians to the very roots of their soul — Alexandrians and therefore intelligent. Alexandrians and therefore heretics, Alexandrians and therefore without illusions. This is what they professed: the road to God is not that of faith, but of knowledge (*gnosis*). Man should not strive to believe, but to know. This world is fundamentally imperfect, depraved and illusory. God is not its father. But every human being possesses a part of His light in his own ill-fashioned, corruptible body, which is destined to become carrion. One must work patiently to free the divine spark from its prison of flesh, patiently blow on the embers until death. Such, said the Gnostics, was the life that true men should live.

They grouped themselves in ascetic communities, performed strange rituals and strove to live outside conventional moralities and established orders, which they believed to be the creation of the almost all-powerful devil. They were the first and the most intransigent dissidents in history sometimes to the point of martyrdom. Their doctrine proved mortal, but not the idea that inspired it: this idea exerts as powerful a hold on men's hearts as the desire to awaken from sleep — it is, despite appearances, of great fortifying power and perfectly libertarian. The heirs of these intractable men often changed their name as the centuries passed, but they never changed their course. They were all those who resolved to hold themselves aloof from base contingencies, never to submit to the petty tyrannies of the ephemeral, and to strive, stubbornly and with a clear purpose, towards absolute knowledge. They were always heretics, outside the law, conscientious objectors.

Do not sleep, the Gnostics would say, but remain in a state of perpetual wakefulness. He who falls asleep is a corpse who does not know himself. He who falls asleep will not become God. One cannot help thinking that, in three thousand years of achievement, ancient Egypt had never said anything different.

The cult of the sun was the cult of the open eye. The legend of death was recited for love of the open eye. Three thousand years of history were written to the glory of the open eye. The strength of the ancient Egyptians was inspired by the firm desire never to close the eye. At Gurnah, near Thebes, in the **tomb of the vizir Ramoseh**, two figures are carved on a wall: a woman is holding a man by the shoulder, feeling his living warmth; she is saying: 'look'. She wants to say: 'do not die'. All the tombs in Egypt are similar prayers to the open eye. Seeing and knowing are related ideas. The distant inhabitants of the 'black land' wished to know, to open the last door of the last divine dwelling at the heart of the interior sun, and to see. All that remains today of their quest is their desire expressed in stone. The pyramids, the mural paintings, the statues and temples are only questions put to the sky. The answer — if there was or is one — does not lie at the centre of their labyrinths, but is buried in some mummified heart, in some vanished spirit, beyond the reach of a scribe's pen.

At the end of the journey, what remains behind the eye? A sublime smile on a stone face, a *felucca* on the Nile, between Luxor and Karnak, an overwhelming forest of columns, a tomato munched in a garden in front of a laughing woman, the minarets of Cairo among the stars — fleeting moments. Through all its gods and its devils Egypt is more alive than all the words in the world. Its ancient monuments are alive because they pose the fundamental questions of living beings. Its people belongs to the sun, it is exasperating, warm, violent, hospitable, peaceable and elusive — and at all costs determined to live. It is like the child encountered in a lane of the Khan el Khalili. He goes barefoot, dressed in a tattered *galabieh*. In one hand he holds a whining old transistor radio, in the other a scarab carved from green stone. 'I'll sell it to you', he says, 'it's a sun.' The traveller smiles and replies: 'What does the radio say?' The child also smiles: 'The war is over, everything's all right, they are talking. I'll swap my scarab for your pen.' The bargain is concluded without futile argument. They go and drink tea in a tiny café. The child disappears for a moment, returns and offers the traveller a small box of red velvet. Inside is a miniature Koran. 'Welcome to Egypt', he says.

He laughs. Nothing is more beautiful than his open eye.

Gurnah. Bas-relief on the tomb of Ramoseh.

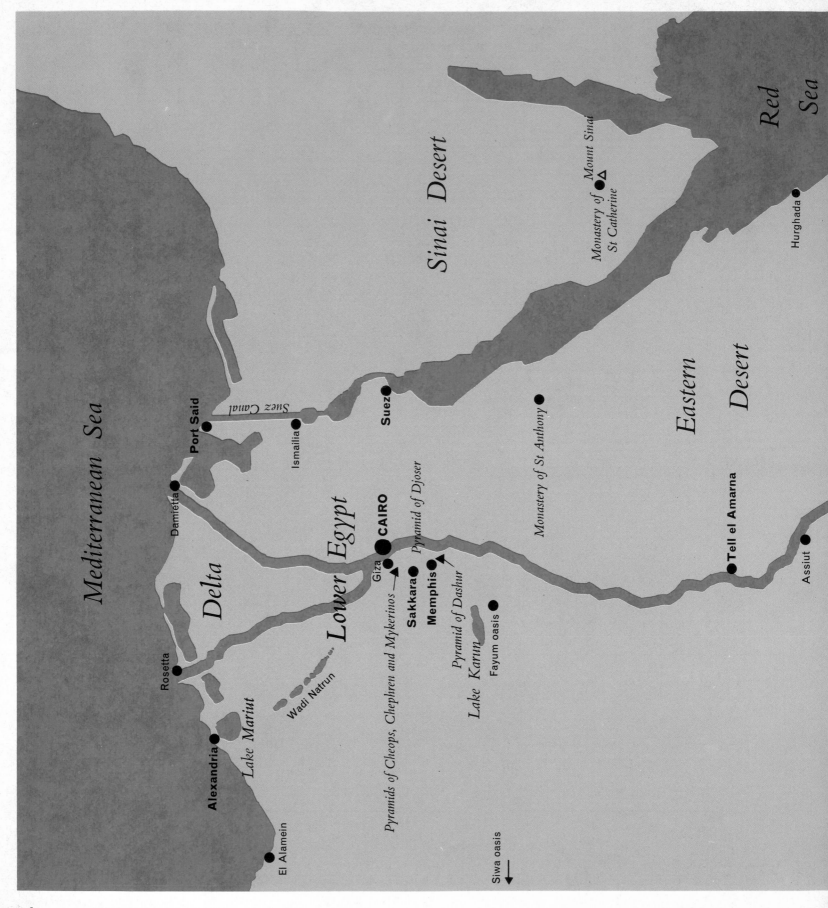

Mediterranean Sea

Red Sea

Sinai Desert

Eastern Desert

Delta

Lower Egypt

Port Said

Damietta

Rosetta

Alexandria

Lake Mariut

El Alamein

Ismailia

Suez

Suez Canal

CAIRO

Giza

Pyramids of Cheops, Chephren and Mykerinos

Sakkara

Memphis

Pyramid of Djoser

Pyramid of Dashur

Lake Karun

Fayum oasis

Wadi Natrun

Siwa oasis

Monastery of St Anthony

Monastery of St Catherine

Mount Sinai

Hurghada

Tell el Amarna

Assiut

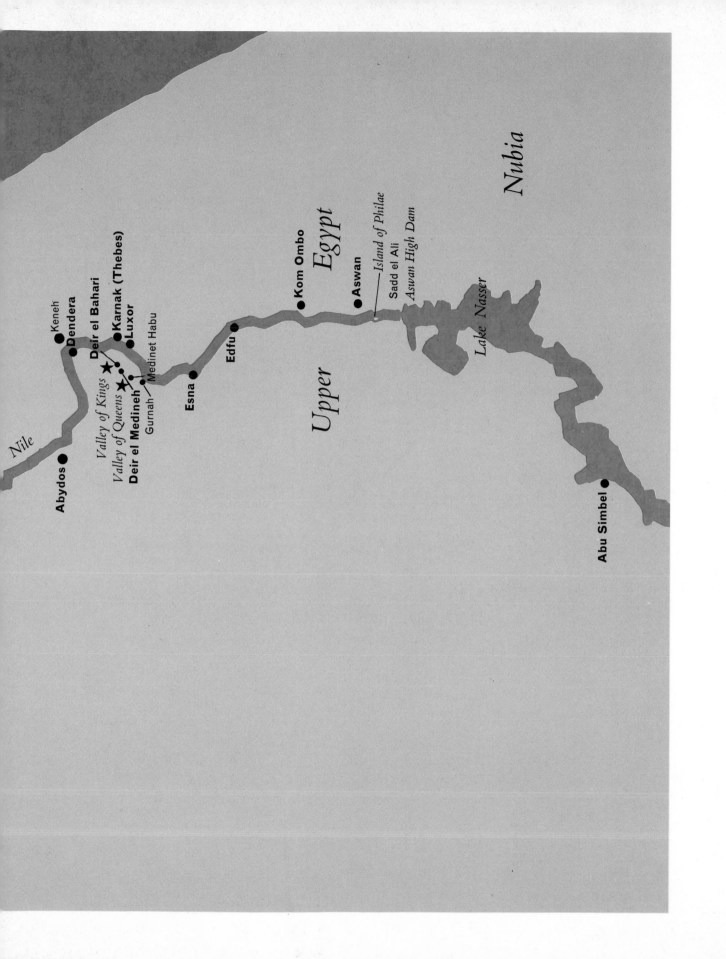

Nile

Keneh

Dendera

Abydos

Deir el Bahari

Valley of Kings

Valley of Queens

Deir el Medineh

Gurnah

Medinet Habu

Karnak (Thebes)

Luxor

Esna

Edfu

Kom Ombo

Aswan

Island of Philae

Sadd el Ali

Aswan High Dam

Upper

Egypt

Nubia

Lake Nasser

Abu Simbel

INFORMATION

THE LONGEST HISTORY IN HISTORY

The history of Egypt is like the Nile. Its source is so remote, its course so complex, its ramifications so unexpected, its sphere of influence in both space and time so vast that it seems at first impossible to embrace it in its totality. One can, however, attempt a simplified summary.

The Egyptians, asserts Herodotus, considered themselves the most ancient people on earth. Nothing has yet invalidated this serene confidence of Pharaoh's subjects, and the prehistoric remains found in the 'black and red land' prove that it was one of the first countries to become inhabited and civilized. This proof is of recent origin. It was in hastily excavating Nubia, destined to flooding by the construction of the Aswan High Dam, that archaeologists were able to uncover large layers of flints, tools and rock-paintings that date from the dawn of human history.

At this time the Sahara did not exist and Egypt was an equatorial land. Mural paintings show men confronted by elephants, rhinoceroses and a world of wild beasts. From the Palaeolithic to the Neolithic period, from rudimentary flint that was carved, refined and engraved, from weapons of war to the tools of peace, the first hunter-gatherers of this part of the world set out on the path that was to lead to the zenith of a civilization.

At the end of the Tertiary period the climate changed. A fault formed in the rocky heights which dominate present-day Egypt. The Nile found its way there and began its long labour of alluvial deposits. The sea receded. Egypt made the transition from an equatorial to a tropical country, and the Nile Valley became an oasis. Immediately the nomads settled there. Soon they were practising agriculture, growing barley and wheat, mastering the arts of pottery, basketwork

and weaving, and even discovering the luxury of cosmetics and jewellery. They had their villages of round huts made of puddled clay or reed and their graves, also round, where the dead were adorned with jewels and surrounded by offerings. Gradually houses and tombs became rectangular. Magic statuettes, simple but already astonishingly lifelike, were placed in the tombs to assure eternal life for the deceased. Sculpture on ivory appeared. Transposed to stone, it gave birth to the bas-relief. The totemic animals of the clans of the different ethnic groups assumed the rank of divinities. The falcon, the dog, the ibis and the scorpion took their places in the future pantheon. The nomads, essentially of Kushite, Hamitic and Semitic origin, had become Egyptians.

Four thousand years before the Christian era the clans regrouped in two kingdoms: the kingdom of the North and the kingdom of the South. The first had as its totem Horus, the falcon-god; the second Set, the god with a head vaguely resembling a greyhound. The Scorpion King is said to have lived at this time, devoting his energies to unification. At the beginning of the third millennium Egyptian art was already of admirable quality, writing sophisticated, the calendar in use, irrigation effective, the laws and the cosmogonies assumed more precise forms, and the mud-brick necropolises heralded the architecture to come. Then King Menes, who may have been the legendary Narmer, appeared on the scene and Egypt, already several thousand years old, entered history under the sign of a fabulous sun. At the time of its ultimate eclipse, three thousand years later, the Gauls were barely emerging from the night. Between Menes, the first historical king, and Cleopatra VII, the last Pharaoh, more than thirty dynasties were in turn to occupy the double throne of Upper and Lower Egypt.

THE THINITE PERIOD
(Ist AND IInd DYNASTIES)
(3200–2780 BC)

Menes and the fifteen kings who, in two dynasties, succeeded him were the real founders of Egypt. Writing was codified, the kingdom organized and the Pharaonic theocracy solidly established. At the axis of the two Egypts was to be built the capital, Memphis ('the white wall').

THE OLD KINGDOM
(IIIrd TO Xth DYNASTY)
(2780–2100 BC)

With the IIIrd dynasty and the Pharaoh Djoser began the Old Kingdom, truly a golden age. The kings did not extend their kingdom or engage in battle — at the most some expeditions to the mines of precious metals — but were content to put their state in order. This was the time of the pyramids. They first appeared at Sakkara, where Imhotep built the magnificent Step Pyramid for Djoser, at Neferka, Unas, Dashur and Meidum (the pyramids of King Snefru), then at Giza where the three great pyramids of Cheops, Chephren and Mykerinos were erected. Unas, a king of the Vth dynasty, had the first known funerary inscriptions (the 'Texts of the Pyramids') en-

graved on the inner walls of his tomb. His successors were to observe the same custom. During this time the builders erected a hundred masterpieces, the sculptors created a thousand marvels. Never was statuary to be as beautiful, simple and vigorous as that which emerged, in wood or stone, from the chisels of the sculptor and which included the Crouching Scribe and Sheikh el Beled. At the same time the organization of the kingdom assumed a more precise form, based on the conditions imposed by nature. The Nile, with its floods, made necessary a unitary, centralized structure which the administration's officials proceeded to build up. The entire country was provided with a network of irrigation works, dykes and bridges. This tremendous effort was accepted in a good spirit by the people, slavery did not exist and social discipline was a matter of consent freely given. The gods of each clan became assimilated one with another and gradually, under different names, came to represent the same divinities of a vast cosmogony. Psychological unity was finally founded on the universality of the myth of Osiris, the king-god who had emerged triumphant from his trials against Set, the god of the barren desert, and of Horus, son of Osiris and Isis, a myth which established the idea of the supremacy of good over evil. Five centuries of peace passed thus, under the benevolent eye of Re.

About the VIth dynasty, however, the skies darkened. The governors of the *nomes* (provinces), the nomarchs, grew restless and challenged the Pharaoh's power and wealth. The royal authority began to crumble. The people revolted and demanded, in addition to bread, the right to the funerary rituals that would enable all men to be reborn as Osiris (hitherto this privilege had been reserved for the king and princes). Anarchy was rampant. Two clans, one at Thebes, the other at Heracleopolis, engaged in a devastating war. It was not until 2100 BC that the Theban clan triumphed and that unity and order were restored.

THE MIDDLE KINGDOM
(XIth TO XVIIth DYNASTY)
(2100–1570 BC)

The former vizir Ammenemes opened the era of the Middle Kingdom. A new period of peace began. Strengthened by past experience, the Pharaohs accorded fewer privileges to the nobles and looked more to the people for support. The plebeian uprising which had destroyed the Old Kingdom had borne its fruit; greater justice prevailed, a genuine social morality was preached and henceforth virtue was to be the sole criterion of admission permitting access to the life beyond, to the brotherhood of the gods. At the same time Egypt had fortified and armed itself. Few architectural traces of the Middle Kingdom remain, for nearly all were re-used in later constructions, notably at Luxor and at Karnak. But the statues, with their infinitely human and melancholy faces, are beautiful, and the minor arts (goldsmith's work, mural paintings) reached peaks of virtuosity.

Then another storm arose. This time it came from a region unmarked by frontiers where only chaos could prevail. The Hyksos, the shepherd-kings from Asia, poured down on Egypt. They possessed a formidable weapon, the horse-drawn chariot. They invaded the Delta and Middle Egypt, plundering, burning, massacring and reducing the population to slavery. The war was to last a hundred years during which the Theban princes, who remained in Upper Egypt beyond the reach of the Hyksos domination, were to attempt to drive out the invader. About 1570 BC, Ahmosis, first king of the XVIIIth dynasty, captured Avaris, the Hyksos capital, won a decisive victory over the Barbarians, restored order and inaugurated the New Kingdom.

THE NEW KINGDOM
(XVIIIth TO XXth DYNASTY)
(1570–1085 BC)

The New Kingdom was to be a period of wars, conquests and permanent contacts with Asia, and it saw the people become increasingly servile, ill-treated and impoverished. However, it was also a period in which the Pharaohs, in a mighty burst of activity, as if they felt their civilization shuddering, were to indulge in a frenzy of building, for their own glory and for that of their gods. It was now that the most beautiful temples of Karnak, at Luxor and in the Valley of Kings rose up from the sands. The New Kingdom witnessed the reigns of Tuthmosis, the Pharaoh-queen Hatshepsut (1504–1482) who had the beautiful temple of Deir el Bahari built, Amenophis III (1408–1372) who brought Karnak to its greatest glory, Akhenaten (1372–1362) who built Tell el Amarna, Tutankhamun and, above all, Ramesses II (1304–1237). This last great Pharaoh fought against the Hittites and the Assyrians, claimed to be the master of Africa and Asia, and tirelessly ordered the construction of the granite colossi, obelisks and temples that were to earn him immortality, among them the stupendous monuments of Abu Simbel.

THE LATE PERIOD
(XXIst TO XXXth DYNASTY)
(1085–332 BC)

However, all this building effort, the wars, the opulent life of the Pharaohs and the excessive power of the priests, who had gained control of financial and temporal matters, had undermined the foundations of Egyptian civilization. An inevitable decadence began. In the XXth dynasty, after the assassination of Ramesses III, anarchy prevailed. The priests of Amun ruled at Thebes. A royal dynasty established itself at Tanis, in the Delta, where the Libyans assumed power. Then Egypt was split up into little kingdoms which were conquered by the king of Kush (the present-day Sudan) and, in the XXVth dynasty, came under the rule of the Kushite (or Ethiopian) dynasty, while Thebes was twice sacked by the Assyrians. About 663 BC the Kushites were defeated by the princes of Sais, and the Saites established the XXVIth dynasty. These kings turned to Greece, which had long been fascinated by Egypt, and Egypt became Mediterranean. In the meantime the Persian threat became increasingly forceful and finally triumphed. In 524 BC Cambyses ravaged Egypt. Darius, in spite of his greater moderation and benevolence, failed to win the loyalty of the Egyptians. Between two battles

against the Persians, the last three 'native' dynasties made a last effort to restore the temples and to build new ones, at Esna, Dendera and Philae, as if they wanted to leave a testament behind them, but they were unable to avoid disintegration. In 342 BC Egypt once again came under the rule of the Persians. Its liberator, Alexander the Great, was Greek. He proved benevolent and tolerant, founded Alexandria and departed. When the kingdom was divided up, the Ptolemies occupied the throne of the Pharaohs. The first king, the general Ptolemy Lagos, who governed Egypt from the time of the conqueror's death, gave his name to the dynasty of the Lagides. Egypt had become Greek; it was to remain Greek for four centuries officially and for a thousand years culturally.

THE PTOLEMIES
(332–30 BC)

The Ptolemies left the administrative power in the hands of the priests and officials, but took a firm hold of military and economic matters. With their coming the native class disappeared; it was not to be restored until the present century. Under their rule, which was gentle, tolerant and enlightened, the peasants were left to their planting, the scribes to their book-keeping, the people and clergy to their life of servility. The 'Greek colonials' alone enjoyed full rights of Egyptian citizenship, they had their own laws and owned the best lands. The colonized Egyptians were subject to a Greek administration, were allowed to cultivate the lands of the state (the least fertile) only by concession, and had to hand over to the administration a third of their harvest. Alexandria, the new capital of the Mediterranean, was not their city. Egypt clung desperately to its religion and to its past, and for the rest ceased to be. When, after the defeat of Cleopatra VII and Antony at Actium in 30 BC, it passed into the hands of the Romans and became administratively a Roman province, the 'granary' of Rome, it would have accepted its fate with perfect indifference if the plundering of its treasures and the poverty of its people had not been intensified.

The Roman Empire grew, prospered and declined. Egypt no longer existed. When Christianity came, it spoke of justice and peace to an oppressed people. The Egyptians, who had never venerated the Greco-Roman gods, were drawn towards the Christian God, and they were to have their martyrs. Then, when Christianity had finally established itself, their patriarchs, who were to be the new masters of the country during the Byzantine Empire, played a brilliant part in the successive Councils of the Church. But this Christian world was troubled by endless theological quarrels. Heresy, struggles for power, economic factors — all became intermingled. The Byzantine Empire dismissed, exiled and murdered the heretical patriarchs, replacing them with orthodox patriarchs who, at the same time, were appointed administrators of Egypt. The Egyptians, who believed themselves saved by Christianity, had suffered their final disillusionment. Thus, when the Arabs arrived, they offered no resistance. After having been Pharaonic, Greek, Roman and Christian, why should Egypt not become Muslim? It became Muslim and was to remain so.

THE HOUR OF ISLAM

In AD 640 the fate of Egypt became identified with that of Islam. Liberty or persecution, war or peace, prosperity or poverty, all depended on the distant caliphs represented by the governors whom they delegated to rule the land. These governors were sometimes Turks, sometimes Arabs, sometimes Kurds. From time to time they would sever the bond which tied them to their masters in an attempt to rule independently. They were sometimes tolerant, sometimes intolerant, sometimes upright, dynamic and enlightened, at other times merely treasure-seekers intent on enriching either the caliph or themselves.

THE OMMAYYADS

The Ommayyads were the first Muslim dynasty to reign over Egypt. Twenty years earlier, at Mecca, the junction of the great caravan routes and an important centre of pagan pilgrimage, a prophet, Mohammed had preached a new, monotheist religion to the Bedouins. In 622 he had been forced to flee with his followers and establish himself at Medina. This was the 'hegira' ('flight'), the beginning of the Muslim era. Ten years later Mohammed, now all powerful, returned to Mecca, demolished the idols and inaugurated the cult of Allah. Islam was born. Mohammed died without leaving an appointed successor. Four caliphs were elected in turn to carry the torch. The last, Ali, husband of Fatima, the Prophet's daughter, was assassinated. The governor of Syria, Moawiya, seized power, established his capital at Damascus and made provision for an hereditary succession. He was a Sunnite (sunna means 'tradition') and opposed to the followers of Ali's descendants, who would not recognize him as their master and were called Shiites. Moawiya founded the Ommayyad dynasty which, from 660 to 750, was to lead the Islamic empire to its greatest glories. Egypt played an important role, serving as a revictualling base for the Arab conquerors. It taught them something of which they were ignorant — navigation. In their wisdom the first Arab rulers left the administration and its body of Christian officials as they were. They allowed freedom of worship. But they imposed a heavy tax (the poll-tax) on all non Muslims. In consequence, conversions took place at a rapid rate. Since the Koran could not be translated, the use of Arabic was enforced. By the end of the seventh century the Christians were a minority and Arabic had become the official, administrative language. All would have gone well if taxes had not become increasingly punitive. When they weighed too heavily, the Copts ('Copt' being the Arabic translation of the Greek word *egyptoi*) revolted and the bloody cycle of repressions began.

In 750 a movement originating in Iran caused the downfall of the Ommayyad dynasty. The Abbasids, who moved their capital from Damascus to Baghdad, became the new masters. Baghdad enjoyed a dazzling reputation, but the army was unreliable. The caliph therefore reinforced it with Turkish slaves, and these mercenaries were to assume an increasing importance, gradually eliminating the Arab element.

THE TIME OF IBN TULUN

In 868 a Turkish general, Ibn Tulun, took control of the government of Egypt. He broke with Baghdad and ruled alone. Managing Egypt's affairs with wisdom and honesty, he built in Cairo the beautiful mosque that bears his name. He became so popular that he was able to transform his temporary power into an hereditary power, the Tulunid dynasty. But the son did not possess his father's qualities, and in 905 the Tulunid dynasty was dead. The caliph of Baghdad reassumed power, but for barely thirty years. In 935 Ikhshid, the descendant of a Turkish guard, became in turn the independent ruler of Egypt. He left the spiritual domain to the caliph, but appropriated the temporal power and reigned over Egypt, Syria, the Yemen and the Holy Cities, founding the Ikhshidid dynasty. The regent who was to govern on his death, an Abyssinian eunuch named Kafur, made Fustat (Old Cairo) a flourishing cultural centre.

On Kafur's death the supporters of Ali, who had never recognized the Sunnites, drove them out and seized power. They were known as the Fatimids, from the name Fatima. They took possession of Egypt without striking a blow, granted it independence, converted it on a massive scale to the Shiite rite, although the Sunnites were not persecuted, and gave it an era of prosperity. They developed Alexandria, in its death throes, and above all founded Cairo which rapidly assumed declining Baghdad's position of supremacy in the Islamic world. The university-mosque of El Azhar was founded and became the theological centre of Islam. For a century the Fatimids remained in power. But they in their turn were forced to have recourse to foreign troops. A period of famine came and the Fatimids collapsed, confronted by the insurrection of the mercenaries and by the Turks, the champions of orthodox Islam who were threatening them on one side while the Crusaders were attacking them on the other.

THE TIME OF SALADIN

In 1164 Nur el Din attempted to reunite the Muslims against the Crusaders. When Egypt appealed to him for help, he sent his lieutenant Salah el Din (Saladin), who defeated the Crusaders, freed himself from the tutelage of Nur el Din and inaugurated the Ayyubid dynasty. He built the citadel that surrounds Cairo and Fustat, governed with wisdom and undertook major building works that included not only military defences but also hospitals and centres of education. Through him and his descendants Egypt enjoyed another period of revival, until 1250. However, at the time when St Louis was a prisoner in Egypt, the Turkish militia with which the Ayyubids had surrounded themselves massacred their masters and seized power.

THE REIGN OF THE MAMELUKS

The Mameluks, the Turkish mercenaries, had brought chaos to the country once again. Immediately after their seizure of power, however, they began to work for the prosperity and greatness of Egypt and established the 'Muslim peace', the equivalent of the Pax Romana. The throne of Egypt became the throne of Islam and, according to some historians, the Mameluk period was the most brilliant in medieval history.

At the end of the fifteenth century the Mameluks were to fall in their turn, for economic reasons — the discovery of the maritime route round the Cape of Good Hope which ruined Egypt. The Ottomans installed themselves in their place and to administer Egypt appointed governors or *pashas*, who changed every year and were totally uninterested in the country. Again Egypt plunged into poverty, at a time when it was becoming the object of rivalries between France, Russia and Britain. With Bonaparte's expedition in 1798, France won the first round at the Battle of the Pyramids, where the last Mameluks were defeated. An era had ended. Modern Egypt then proceeded slowly to emerge from its accumulated ashes.

THE ARRIVAL OF MEHEMET ALI

Bonaparte had succeeded only in overthrowing the oligarchy of the last Mameluks and the Ottomans. Shortly afterwards an Albanian soldier of fortune, Mehemet Ali, arrived, having been dispatched to Egypt by Constantinople to wage war against the French. The French were driven out, with the aid of the British, the Mameluks were annihilated, and Mehemet Ali took advantage of the vacuum of power, played on rivalries, presented himself to the people as a liberator and unifier, and had himself elected *pasha* of Cairo. He rebuilt the Egyptian state, laid the foundations of a prosperous economy, encouraged cotton growing, collaborated with the French to reorganize Egypt's industrial equipment and founded a dynasty that was to endure until Farouk, the last king. In spite of the state capitalism he inaugurated, confiscating all wealth for himself, as the Pharaohs had done, he accomplished a remarkable feat and re-established all the virtues of tolerance and open-mindedness which have always characterized the Egyptians. Thanks to him, the peasants' income tripled between 1853 and 1890, as did their birth-rate. His direct descendants, Ibrahim Pasha, Said and Ismail, succeeded him. Ismail was imprudent. In order to complete the construction of the Suez Canal, opened in 1869, he accumulated debts to the point of bankruptcy. In 1882 Britain, the principal creditor, sought satisfaction by imposing on Egypt a *de facto* protectorate which several years later was to become an official protectorate and was to last until 1922, not without many a bloody revolt.

THE WAFD AND THE BIRTH OF MODERN EGYPT

The British protectorate weighed heavily on Egypt, although Britain was mainly concerned with administration and with the production of the cotton that was so useful to the mills of Manchester. During the First World War, moreover, a severe burden of contribution was laid on Egypt's shoulders. In 1918 a group of Egyptian patriots determined to obtain national independence went as a delegation (*wafd*) to put their views to the British High Commission, but in vain. The *Wafd*, however, under the leadership of Saad Zaghlul Pasha, became a mighty nationalist movement. It was not until 1922 that it obtained satisfaction on the form of an agreement, and only in 1936 that it secured the substance of that agreement: the real withdrawal, though only partial, of British troops. In 1922 King Fuad became the first independent sovereign of modern Egypt. His son Farouk succeeded him in 1936. Both governed by leaning sometimes on the *Wafd*, which had become the first political party, and sometimes on the British. Once again, Egypt was sick with unemployment, poverty, a galloping birth-rate and a rural sub-proletariat that was to swell the number of the poor in the large towns. The situation had become explosive. In 1948 a first conflict with Israel erupted, and Egypt suffered a harsh defeat. There was revolt, bitterness and destitution. The people grumbled and created disturbances. In 1952 the conflagration occurred, as clashes took place between Egyptians and British in the Canal Zone. The British artillery caused a massacre. Cairo was set on fire as hotels, cinemas and cafés were burned down. Farouk, corrupt, useless and powerless, could do nothing. On 23 July 1952 a group of young officers who had been preparing themselves in the shadows seized power, led by Gamal Abdel Nasser. Farouk was exiled and the Republic proclaimed the following year. The first action of these peasant officers, whose average age was thirty-five, was to announce agrarian reform. Then they attacked the British, who were still in possession of the Suez Canal. In 1954 the last British troops left Egypt. Nasser turned first to the West, but he did not receive the welcome he had hoped for and, in particular, found himself denied the loans that would enable him to build the Aswan High Dam, in his view the only solution that would ensure Egypt's survival. He then veered towards the countries of the East. In 1956 he nationalized the Suez Canal, which provoked immediate reprisals from the Western bloc. The Egyptian reply was the confiscation and nationalization of all foreign property and a massive exodus of French, British and Jews. Nasser became the leader of Arab nationalism. In 1958 he proclaimed the union of Egypt with Syria under the name of the United Arab Republic, but the union was never to assume a concrete form.

On 28 September 1970, at the age of fifty-two, Nasser died of a heart attack. He was succeeded by Anuar el Sadat, who in a different, less austere style has sought to re-establish contacts with the Western world — with the Americans in particular — and has made the political system more flexible. In the meantime, the fire that had been kindled in the Middle East with the birth of Israel burst into flame from time to time: in 1956 the Sinai campaign, in 1967 the Six Day War, each occasion resulting in an Egyptian defeat. In 1973 a new war broke out. This time Egypt gained some important victories which, in its own eyes, restored its dignity.

Since then, in a time of neither war nor peace, negotiations have followed a narrow, tortuous and interminable path. which has led most recently to the historic conference of Sadat, Begin and Carter in the USA at Camp David. But the

Egyptian people themselves, far from the green carpets of international politics, speak only of peace and friendship. Five thousand years old, the 'black and red land' is inhabited by twenty-year-old men. First Nasser and then Sadat have given them a voice, words and hope. Their future lies before them.

EGYPT IN THE WEST

Diane Harlé, born into a family originating from Minia in the heart of Egypt, was a painter and sculptress before devoting herself to the history of art and specializing in Egyptian archaeology. On the staff of the Department of Egyptian Antiquities at the Louvre since 1958, she is also a lecturer at national museums and an assistant lecturer at the Ecole du Louvre. She took part in the 'Tutankhamun and his epoch' exhibition and also in the 'Ramesses the Great' exhibition in 1976.

The Department of Egyptian Antiquities at the Louvre resembles the land of the Pharaohs: a vast, sober ground floor, like the desert, and a colourful, patchwork first floor like the fertile fields of Egypt. In this exalted place specially arranged for the man who came to be known as 'the Egyptian', the first curator of the Department's collections, Jean-Francois Champollion, brought together in 1826 a mass of handicraft treasures which are today regarded as works of art, and which only the inventive spirit of a civilization rich in principles could have created. It is by reference to the most outstanding of these masterpieces and those of comparable museums that this article attempts to sketch a brief picture of the art through which the most ancient civilization in history expressed itself.

Pharaonic art is essentially religious. 'Art for art's sake' did not exist, each artist and craftsman worked for the glory of the Pharaoh, the guarantor and intermediary between the gods and man, and also the incarnation of god on earth. This is why the majority of objects displayed in museums originated from temples and tombs and, more rarely, from royal or civil dwellings.

Egypt being a privileged land as far as stone is concerned, the sculptors used granite, sandstone, limestone, schist and alabaster. They also used local woods, the acacia and the palm tree, or woods imported from Lebanon or from central Africa, such as cedar and ebony. Ivory, bone and copper were also to be employed, but iron appeared only at a late stage, towards the end of the second millennium BC. Bronze, known since at least 3000 BC, was to be a favourite product from 1000 BC onwards. The artists covered these materials with plaster or stucco and painted them to give greater life to the surface. Various decorative elements were inlaid.

PREHISTORY

The traces of the first Egyptians must be sought on the high plateaux, today desert land, that border the Nile Valley. Vestiges of the 'Pebble Culture', the first 'hominians', have recently been discovered to the west of Thebes, making it possible to date man's first appearance in Egypt as over one-and-a-half million years BC; but all that remains are a few centres of Palaeolithic craftwork which appeared long afterwards. Stone implements and rock-drawings are, at present, the only heritage of these 'cavemen' whose rock shelters provided both a habitation and protection. From the beginning of the Neolithic age the inhabitants of the Nile relinquished their nomadic life for a sedentary existence and settled in the valley of the Nile to cultivate the soil which, every year, received its new layer of fertile silt.

Flint weapons reflect some of the stages which prehistoric man passed through, from the flaked flint, the Palaeolithic pick from the Thebes region, to the little saw (age of polished stone) and the axe of polished jadeite. In the Neolithic period the technique of flint-working was perfected, and regularly shaped arrowheads lie scattered over the terraces dominating the Nile Valley, together with the 'fish-tail' lance points, the 'laurel-leaf' blades and the large knives of light coloured flint characteristic of the Neolithic civilization, with handles made of bone or ivory, like the famous knife from Gebel el Arak, now in

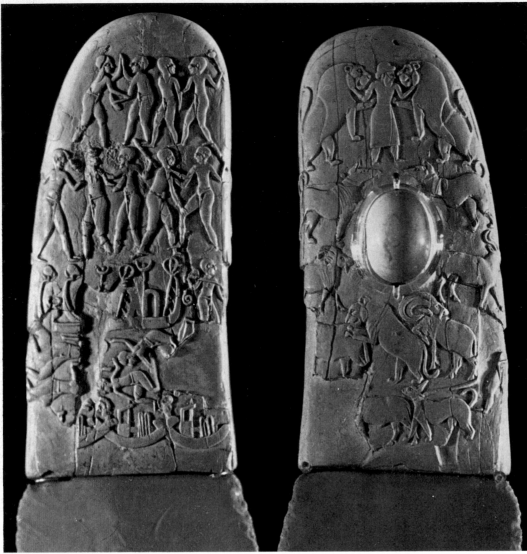

The two sides of the knife from Gebel el Arak.

stalled. The term 'Thinite', used to refer to the first two dynasties, comes from the word 'This', the name of the chief city of the eighth *nome* of Upper Egypt and the capital of the new kings. The location of the kings' capital is not known for certain. Their place of burial is also something of a problem: up to the present time it was thought that their necropolis was at Abydos, the sacred city of the god Osiris situated not far from This, but the recent excavations at Sakkara in Lower Egypt indicate that here too there existed a vast necropolis where the names of the sovereigns of the first and second dynasties have been found; this discovery suggests that Memphis, built at the tip of the Delta, might have been their capital. It is now thought by most scholars that Abydos was the real place of interment for these kings, while at Sakkara were buried many of their high officials. The stele of a king whose name was written with the serpent sign read Djet Uadji, now in the Louvre, probably formed part of the funerary ensemble belonging to his burial at Abydos. The delicately carved ivory figure of a Thinite king wearing a cloak, also found at Abydos, may be seen in the British Museum.

Ivory statuettes of the 'concubine' type show that, from the beginning of the history of Egypt, sculpture in the round was a means of expression for this people so rich in artistic creativity. One fine example, carved and painted, from Abydos is now housed in the Metropolitan Museum.

OLD KINGDOM

(2780-2258 BC)

In the Old Kingdom, not far from the capital Memphis, the pyramids rose up from the sand as if launching an assault on the sky. From the hills of Abu Roash to those of Illahun lie the eternal dwellings of the kings of the IIIrd, IVth, Vth and VIth dynasties, and also the pyramids of the pharaohs of the Middle Kingdom. These artificial mounds, surrounded by the tombs of *mastabas* or their wives, their children and their courtiers formed a complex ensemble with the temple in the valley and the high temple (funerary temple) erected against the east face of the pyramid.

The royal portrait, although idealized (Pharaoh was god on earth), is represented by works of sensitive treatment and perfect finish like the sphinx's head of Radjedet (IVth dynasty) in the Louvre. Equally impressive is the free-standing group of King Mycerinus and his queen now in the Boston Museum of Fine Arts (IVth Dynasty). The gesture of the queen who clasps her husband in no way detracts from the majestic quality of this pair statue. The civil statuary of the IIIrd dynasty presents a rougher style than that of the royal statuary. The statues of Sepa and his wife Nesa also in the Louvre indicate that the artist had not yet succeeded in wholly freeing himself from the block of stone. The head is buried in the shoulders, the smile fixed and the attitude stiff. In direct contrast are the two wooden statues of the Councillor Mitry and his wife to be found in the Metropolitan Museum. The two statues are entirely free-standing and exhibit both remarkable workmanship and a rare ability to convey the dignity of such an official.

the British Museum, or sometimes covered with engraved gold-leaf.

Pottery, originally without ornamentation, was gradually to evolve in the Neolithic period. Engraved decoration made way for the red vases with black rims, formed without the aid of the potter's wheel, which in turn were to be replaced by vessels of hard stone such as diorite, basalt and granite. Certain shapes, on a stem, may have been contemporary with the El Obeid period in Mesopotamia (about 5000 BC); others, with a rounder bulge, have little handles through which cords could be passed — this latter type was to be continued into the historic period. Several of these bowls of hard stone, only a few millimetres in thickness, show the skill of the craftsmen of prehistoric Egypt and are genuine masterpieces. The motifs decorating some vessels, painted on a whitish ground and of great technical perfection, resemble those found on the walls of an underground edifice built in the old city of Hierakonpolis.

The schist palettes used for grinding the traditional colours in the Neolithic period were also to undergo a great transformation. At first they were round or rectangular; then they assumed the forms of fishes with inlaid eyes, tortoises, and birds, or shield-shaped plates with birds' heads at the top. Towards the beginning of the historic period appeared the first decorated palettes: the bas-relief was born with all the characteristics and conventions which artists were to follow for three thousand years. Animal motifs and hunting scenes surround the cup in the centre of the palette used for grinding cosmetic colours. Typical examples of this style are the so-called Hunters' Palette in the British Museum, which shows warriors hunting; and a palette in the Metropolitan Museum of Art in New York where the central cup is formed by a coiled serpent surrounded by various animals. These palettes also bear the first known hieroglyphic signs.

THINITE PERIOD

(3200-2780 BC)

It can be supposed that by the beginning of the Thinite period the unification of Egypt was complete and that a monarchic system had been in-

The painted statue of a seated scribe in the Louvre is one of the most remarkable works of the later Old Kingdom. The artist seems to have caught a living likeness of the expression and gesture of this high official in the process of writing. The inlaid eyes are formed of a band of engraved copper in which is set the white stone of the crystalline lens and the cone of rock-crystal representing the iris.

In the same period, in addition to the bas-reliefs on the tombs and to strengthen their magic power, so that the deceased might be further guaranteed all the food he would require in the afterlife, statuettes or models of tombs representing brewers and bread-makers are carved in the limestone, depicting simple activity in the service of the dead. Particularly vivid representations of a brewer straining mash or of a woman grinding grain may be found in the Metropolitan Museum.

The funeral offering can also take the form of a stele. The stele of the lady Nefertiabet is one of the most marvellous examples of the genre and of the art of relief at the beginning of the VIth dynasty. In the Vth dynasty the bas-relief became an essential element of the architecture which it animated. The coloured reliefs and paintings on the tombs of Sakkara are well illustrated at the Louvre; those of Akhtihetep and Metheti are highly appealing, both from the artistic point of view and for their historical interest, for these works give an idea of the administration of the country and of its daily life. A relief from the tomb of Ptahsekhemankh now in the Boston Museum shows a typical agricultural scene: men ploughing with oxen, workers cutting grain and driving donkeys to the threshing floor. Scenes from the tomb of Urirenptah now housed in the British Museum show musicians at the funerary feast and the preparation of the deceased man's bed. Sarcophagi are represented by huge limestone blocks, the most beautiful of which were adorned with the motif of the archaic wall with redans.

The minor arts are represented by mirrors, bowls and copper ewers, the latter often reproducing the stone or fine pottery forms of the Old Kingdom. Particularly interesting are the model bowls and altar in copper from the tomb of a priest, Idy, now in the British Museum.

FIRST INTERMEDIATE PERIOD, MIDDLE KINGDOM, SECOND INTERMEDIATE PERIOD
(2258–1570 BC)

After a first intermediate period, when the royalty was disputed and the governors of the Egyptian provinces (the 'nomarchs') seized power for themselves, Egypt regained its hegemony under a Theban king, Mentuhotep. But it was under the kings of the XIIth dynasty, who called themselves Amenemhat or Sesostris, that an artistic renewal made itself felt in the royal workshops.

If the statues of the chancellor Nakhti and of Hapidjefai in the Louvre display a wooden statuary in a provincial style full of vigour but still naive, in contrast the royal statuary of the Theban region marks a new stage in the art of the portrait. The artists were to portray the pharaohs at the different ages of their lives. The vigour of the style, and even the often brutal realism, are new features of the XIIth dynasty which were to supplant the idealist school of Memphis and give birth in the South to works that include the mask and the statues of Sesostris III in youth and in old age. Exceptionally fine is the representation of Sesostris as a sphinx in the Metropolitan Museum, and three statues of the same king in the British Museum.

Female statuettes, hippopotamuses covered with a turquoise blue enamel known as 'Deir el Bahari blue', and a few pieces of gold jewellery are unfortunately too rare examples of the minor arts of this period, for their execution is of exceptional quality.

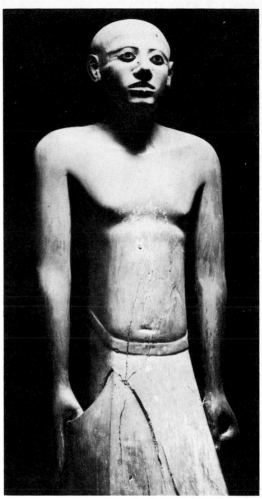

The chancellor Nakhti.

NEW KINGDOM
(1570–1085 BC)

The New Kingdom was a sort of Renaissance that followed the obscurantism of the Hyksos invasion. It was the era of the great conquerors, Tuthmosis III, Amenophis II and Ramesses II, and also of the great idealists and innovators, Hatshepsut, Amenophis III and Amenophis IV-Akhenaten. The stone memorials to their greatness are still to be seen from the Delta to Nubia, not forgetting Thebes 'of the hundred gates'. Their art resembles them. In the temples, palaces and underground chambers remain the traces of a sumptuous decoration.

A work which remains classical in many of its elements, but which above all heralds the revolutionary art of El Amarna in the sensual shaping of the mouth, is the magnificent grey black granite head of Amenophis III in the Louvre. Two fragments, both in the Metropolitan Museum, illustrate the development of this treatment. One has been attributed to Queen Tiyi, the other to Queen Nefretiti.

The statue of Amenophis IV-Akhenaten is a strange image, belonging to a group of twenty or so statues of this king found on the site of the temple of Gen Pa Aten, to the east of the enclosure wall of the temple of Amun at Karnak. This

The Lady Nesa.

king with the emaciated face, long nose, fleshy lips and disproportionately prominent chin, whose inner expression emanating from the half-closed eyelids corresponds perfectly with the mystique he imposed on himself, has vanished from Egyptian history because he bore too great a love for his 'one and only god', the solar deity Aten.

In the Louvre the figure of the lady Teye, high priestess of the god Min at Thebes, measuring thirty-four centimetres, in another wonderful piece of bravura on the part of an artist who lived a little over three thousand years ago. It is beautifully carved in a hard wood with the aid of archaic tools. A similar statuette also in hard wood of the lady Teye may be seen in the Metropolitan Museum. Despite its small size (only twenty-four centimetres high) all the details of an elaborate wig, jewellery and costume drapery have been delicately modelled.

In the XIXth dynasty a clear change transforms the style of the relief. In its concern with perfection it loses something of its vigour and becomes a little too academic. Nevertheless, the painted reliefs of the tomb of Sethi I in western Thebes, now housed in the Louvre, are among the most outstanding in the long history of Egypt: the relief of Sethi I and the goddess Hathor, who wears a highly decorated robe, is quite remarkable.

Painting followed the same development as the art of relief, and the royal structures of El Amarna have bequeathed a collection of works with a bucolic character that corresponds precisely with the principle of returning to sources and to reality which Akhenaten had imposed on himself; among these is a small glass plate representing a calf frisking among a vegetation palpitating with life. The painting in the civilian tombs of the New Kingdom evolved in the same manner as art in general. At the beginning of the XVIIIth dynasty the design was conventional and the colouring reduced to a simple, unsubtle palette, as can be seen in the paintings of the tomb of Unsu. By the middle of the dynasty, however, considerable advance had been made. The fowling scene from the tomb of Nebamun in Thebes, now in the British Museum, illustrates considerable skill with the brush in the rendering of the fur of a cat and the details of butterflies and birds.

The influence of Mycenae and the East is evident in gold jewellery. The forms are more extravagant, the choice of colours more varied; a break had been made with the jewellery of the preceding periods. Nevertheless, from the collections in the Louvre, one can see a link with the Middle Kingdom in a bracelet of small lapis-lazuli beads and gold which is in contrast with the broad bracelet of *cloisonné* gold representing stylized flowers in the purest Cretan and Mycenaean style. A gold ring, with two little horses at a feeding-trough, is a masterpiece of workmanship in itself, as is the pendant inlaid with stones and coloured glass in the form of a winged ram. The Metropolitan Museum houses the magnificent jewellery from the tomb of three queens of Tuthmosis III, in Western Thebes. The collection of bracelets, collars and headdresses in delicately worked gold and inlay testify to the ability of court artisans at this time. Rings set with a scarab or simply cornelian, and also the gold chains with a fish or a lotus as their clasp ornament, remain in the Egyptian tradition. In this same Pharaonic style is the cup of the general Thutii in the Louvre, in chased gold decorated with reliefs of fish and papyrus flower clusters.

The wooden toilet articles made by the craftsmen of the New Kingdom are masterpieces of taste and ingenuity and are worthy of attention. Figures of swimming women cling to the feet of ducks, whose body with detachable wings served as a receptacle for the cosmetic materials. Large-toothed combs of light coloured wood surmounted by a crouching ibex, and the kohl pots in the form of a palm-shaped capital sometimes held by a little monkey, are among the most original examples. The vases and receptacles of the New Kingdom are related to those of earlier periods, both in form and in material, including painted pottery, faience and glass. The stone or wood sarcophagi were becoming anthropomorphic and are richly decorated with funerary vignettes.

DECLINE

In the declining centuries of its history ancient Egypt, weakened by political struggles, was to suffer the yoke of foreign powers, but at the same time its native religion remained firmly rooted. There were no more monumental works, but for the time being art was to preserve the grace characteristic of the New Kingdom. Among the masterpieces of this period are in the Louvre the gold necklace with small bells belonging to King

Amenophis IV-Akhenaten.

Queen Karomama.

Pinudjem I, the triad of Osorkon and the beautiful bronze statuette of the divine worshipper Karomama (XXIInd dynasty) inlaid with gold, silver and electrum.

Unfortunately the XXVth dynasty has left few examples of its art; the precious monument of the Nubian king Taharqa and the god Hemen suggests that the royal workshops still enjoyed a certain prestige which gave a final flourish of brilliance to the so-called Saite XXVIth dynasty. Indeed the granite sphinx of Taharqa, now in the British Museum, is regarded as one of the finest works of this period. Then, with a kind of nostalgia, the artists turned back to the sources of Antiquity; the models they chose go back to the Old and Middle Kingdoms, as can be seen in the statue of the kneeling Nakhthorheb. It was also in the Saite period that Egypt saw the beginnings of a style of portraiture that was certainly to influence the so-called 'realistic' Roman sculpture. The sculptor worked with the hardest stones to portray faces marked by the scars of the age.

The development of animal art was another important phase of this period, for the use of bronze facilitated artistic creativity in this field. The Pharaonic craftsmen, having acquired a perfect mastery of this material, made statuettes of cats representing the goddess Bastet, Apis bulls, ibises, dog-headed figures personifying the god Thoth, and the goose of the god Amun — a whole animal-world that suggest a sort of idolatry, replacing the deities in the minds of believers. These naturalistic figures are so perfectly stylized that one can understand the great vogue that they enjoyed as objects of worship.

At the end of the Pharaonic era vessels in classical forms became more rare and were replaced by glass, which, with age, often produces an iridescent effect. The prototypes of these objects undoubtedly came from Phoenicia. Finally, the bindings of brightly coloured beads were replaced by the painted shrouds and stucco masks that covered mummies from the time of the Greco-Roman invasion. D.H.

ADVICE FROM AN EGYPTIAN

Born in Cairo of Egyptian parents of Syro-Lebanese origin and Christian religion. Leila Bellenis was educated in Europe. Far from her home country, she pursued studies in Egyptology; on completing her studies she happily returned to the scenes of her childhood. Now an archaeological guide, she can offer tourists of all nationalities (she speaks six languages fluently) the benefit of her knowledge and love of Egypt's handicrafts and its people.

EGYPTIAN HANDICRAFTS

In Cairo and its districts

To the visitor of today Cairo is a paradoxical city. The capital of the Arab world, it has modelled itself on the typical international city.

To rediscover Islam one must pass through the centre of the city and cross the street that lies along the old canal, the Khalig el Masir, where the most beautiful houses once stood. It was along the Khalig that the French writers Gérard de Nerval and Pierre Loti lived.

The canal was filled in when the Khedive Ismail, on his return from France, decided to make his capital a little Paris. The canal thus became the longest street in Cairo, passing right through the city and dividing modern Cairo from the medieval city studded by domes and minarets and dominated by the hustle and bustle of the *souks*. These scenes evoke memories of the caliphs and sultans of former times.

Situated on the former canal, the Museum of Islamic Art enables one to follow the great periods of Islam, its art and its history. A visit is worthwhile if only because it helps one to see the link between the forms of the past and those of the daily life of today.

As you leave this building, a street humming with life leads to Bab Zonela, a gate that once gave access to the city. This street is lined with shops offering everything necessary for modern life: brooms, buckets, saddle-cloths and harnesses for horses, donkeys and camels, travelling ovens for baking sweet potatoes, little lamps for the Ramadan, bird-cages and so on.

Eventually you come to Bab Zuweila. Opposite its porch is the Khiyameya, once a covered market where tents of coarse canvas are now made. These tents are in common use and are planted in the middle of a street, at weddings and funerals, to serve as a reception room to which only men are admitted. The home is still the woman's domain. On the unbleached canvas brightly coloured fabrics are laid to form traditional arabesques.

To please tourists the craftsmen also make some amusing stitched patchwork scenes. With their needles they create the most familiar images of the Pharaonic era, such as the weighing of the heart or Ramesses on his chariot drawing his bow; they also produce more simple figures — a stubborn little donkey, a patient fisherman or a belly-dancer.

Seven hundred metres away is the Khan el Khalili, still the favourite haunt both of foreign visitors and of the people of Cairo. The humblest womenfolk come here to buy their gold, for their ornaments are still the only possession which belongs to them personally; the women of the world come here to choose their presents.

This *souk*, founded in 1292 by the sultan Ashraf el Khalil on the site once occupied by the tombs of the Fatimid caliphs, is crammed with shops full of attractive articles. One ought to be able to satisfy one's desires by wandering at random into any one of them. There are, however, streets which specialize in particular goods: the 'Street of Gold', the Souk el Nahassine (copper), the shop of blown glassware, the shop of wooden caskets (inlaid with pearl), the specialist in leather goods, *narghilehs*, *galabiehs*, and also some good antique shops.

There is no need to mention addresses. The visitor can find his way around easily enough. If, however, you wish to visit a craftsman at work, a guide is necessary, as the native quarters lie off the beaten track.

The potters of Old Cairo. Legend relates that in Egypt, beside the cataracts, the god Khnum fashioned the first man on the potter's wheel. This belief confers on the creator-god the attributes of the craftsman.

Pottery remains very much alive. In present day Cairo the craftsmen, performing actions as old as the world itself, create objects which still serve the purposes of everyday life. Among these the most indispensable is the water-cooler, a porous vase in which the water cools by evaporation and which is the refrigerator of the poor.

In Old Cairo, on the very site where the Arab conquerors had founded their first capital, Fustat ('the tent'), lie row upon row of ovens in which the potters make these water-coolers by the hundred. In addition to this vase, whose form and use date from the earliest times, everything that is made of clay originates from this place: piping, sinks, pots, bowls and jars. The potters also make (this time for their own pleasure) large numbers of picturesque figurines representing persons in action: a horseman brandishing his sword, a lady carrying her jug on her head, musicians playing their instruments, fanciful figures of persons and animals, simple in their forms and which appeal to popular taste.

Observing a tradition the origin of which is not always known, the potters still make the candle-holder of the *sebough* (the seventh day from birth). This terracotta candle-holder is designed so that candles can be placed in a circle round some amusing personage at the top of which a cockerel is often found; the whole is painted in bright colours. It is on the seventh day from birth that the new-born child must be given a first name. To choose it, a name is written on each candle; then the candles are lit and the doors opened. The little flames, caught in the draught, gradually disappear; the last candle to be extinguished bears the name predestined for the child, the name 'of long life'.

The walk round Old Cairo is included in all the tourist itineraries. The ovens lie beside the road; you can see them as you pass, together with the abundant display of pottery. The pottery is certainly rather fragile, but it is so expressive that anyone who buys it (at ridiculously low prices) will find it one of the most genuine examples of popular craftsmanship.

The gates of Cairo and the glass-blowers. On leaving Fustat, the first Arab capital, you should follow the road that passes through the City of the Dead and leads to the gates of Cairo, Bab el Futtuh and Bab el Nasr, which date from the same time as Bab Zuweila. The city was already known as 'El Qahira' ('the victorious') — Cairo — and is enclosed by protecting walls pierced with gates built in the eleventh century. A walk along the walls provides a view across the City of the Dead; you can also admire the mosque of El Hakem and discover traces of Bonaparte's expedition. His soldiers carved their names on observation towers — you will find written 'Tour Julien', 'Tour Lescale' and so on. At the time these solid bastions served as a powerful centre of resistance. As you come down the majestic steps of the fortress you will notice stones re-used from other structures dating from Pharaonic times.

After the visit to the fortress, to rediscover the life of modern Cairo and see another craftsman in action you can follow a lane situated just opposite Bab el Futtuh. At the top of a small hill are the two ovens of the glass-blowers. The steep climb and the poverty of the area are soon forgotten.

At Fustat the actions of the potter offered a picture of earth being prepared, kneaded and transformed into objects; the glass-blower offers an image of fire. To be present at the making of the slightest object is a treat for the eye.

The potter is quiet and serene. The glass-blower is nervous and feverish; he bites his cheeks and hollows his chest. All this effort produces vases, little pots, glasses, candlesticks, lamps, jugs with curved spouts and numerous fragile articles in various colours — aquamarine, honey, plum, pale green and faint pink.

These objects are rugged and roughly finished, but always have attractive shapes and an unpretentious charm. There is no need to come here to buy them, for they can be found at the market. Nevertheless, the impression left by watching the glass-blower in action remains long in the memory.

At Kerdassa

On the way to the pyramids of Giza you pass on the left a mud road that runs along a canal lined with eucalyptus trees. About eight kilometres away lies Kerdassa.

This village of craftsmen was once a resting-place on the caravan route. Until the beginning of the present century Kerdassa was a prosperous village. It had provided clothing for the Sudan, the inhabitants of the oases and the people of Cairo.

In this hive of activity the craft was passed on from father to son, like some tale of heroic deeds. With the birth of industry Kerdassa was impoverished. To survive the village had to undergo a transformation. The craft organization has changed hands, and the buyers of today are tourists anxious to acquire cotton and silk fabrics made in the country. The former village is no longer inhabited. As soon as you arrive, two shops attract the attention, but visitors do not often stop here to see the craftsmen's work. Everyone rushes into the sale rooms, where you find fabrics and hand-made objects displayed in the chaotic manner of a bazaar: bags with shoulder-straps, carpets, shirts, blankets, bedspreads, cross-stitch embroideries, tablecloths and children's clothing.

The costume of the oasis has travelled far. The traditional garment, formerly embroidered by the women of Siwa (an oasis in the Libyan Desert), is now available to all.

In this Ali Baba's cave, one never finds the same thing twice. It is an image of life and of the local craft tradition, which resembles those plants that spring up in the desert after the slightest fall of rain.

In Upper Egypt

The Valley of Kings inspires the local craftsmen. At Luxor numerous small workshops imitate the broad pectorals, necklaces and scarabs that adorned the bodies of dead Pharaohs and the ancient little statuettes. Alabaster is prettily shaped into cups, vases and ash-trays; the seeds of plants and sandalwood become charming beads which make original ornaments. The prices depend on one's patience in bargaining. Everywhere *galabiehs*, embroidered or plain, are offered to the passer-by.

L.B.

ITTFADAL:
THE LAWS OF HOSPITALITY

If a single human being were to be chosen as an example of the hospitality, warmth, gentleness and that peculiar gaiety — half joy, half melancholy — that is characteristic of the Egyptians, Marie Saada would be that person.

Knock on her door and go into her house. If you are already known to her and she has not seen you for a long time, she will use the pretty phrase: 'Your absence has made me wild.' If you are a stranger, within an hour you will be a friend and will be showered with the repeated '*Ittfadal*', like cool dew. *Ittfadal* means 'Welcome', 'Help yourself', 'Make yourself at home': it is the password of affectionate communication. Even if you are only stopping for a moment, you will be offered coffee *masbout* (with little sugar) or *ziada* (very sweet). If you are invited to her table, she will do you the honour of a very subtle Egyptian cuisine consisting of *baladi* (that is, genuinely Egyptian) dishes that no luxury hotel in Cairo could serve you.

First of all, the *foul*, the national dish eaten by rich and poor, sold by itinerant vendors in the popular districts, and which all Egyptian women know how to cook. It is made with dry fava beans which are soaked for a long time and then cooked for four hours with oil, salt and a handful of red lentils. It is served with a sauce consisting of minced onions, lemon, oil, salt and cumin, and is eaten with hard-boiled eggs.

You will also be able to sample the *kofta*, a ball of minced lamb or beef, with eggs, onions and spices; the *taamia* (or *falafel* as it is known among Alexandrians), a ball of dry white fava beans highly seasoned and served with *tehina*, a delicious sauce of sesame seeds mixed with water and seasoned with lemon, salt and cumin. You will also be treated either to a delicious cabbage, stuffed leaf by leaf with a mixture of minced beef or lamb and rice, with garlic and dry mint, or to a soup of red lentils. You will finish with a dessert consisting of rice, vanilla and cinnamon, the *mihallabiia*, or the dessert of crushed apricot, the *amar el din* ('moon of religion'), which is served on the first evening of the Ramadan.

If you wish to feel truly Egyptian, try the *meloukhia*, a herb soup made with a minced green vegetable similar to spinach, peppers, coriander and a lot of garlic. This green broth is served with warm rice and slices of fowl. The Egyptians adore this dish, but it sometimes has a highly disconcerting effect on foreigners.

To avoid causing Marie Saada even the slightest trouble, do not add salt to your food and never

Marie Saada — in Arabic her name means 'happiness' — was born at Tantah, the seventh largest town in Egypt, between Cairo and Alexandria, with a population of two hundred and forty thousand.

empty your plate completely. She would see this as a sign that you had not eaten enough. Do not refuse a second helping, for that would mean that the dish was not good. Do not admire any of her possessions too openly, otherwise she would immediately offer it to you without worrying about the object's value, and this would lead to a very subtle battle of politeness.

After dinner she may teach you to play *taola*, a sort of backgammon, or *koukin*, which is similar to rummy.

When you leave, whatever the time is, she will protest: '*Lessa badri!*' (It is too early!'), but you will be able to thank her with the old formula reserved for the very best cooks: 'May God preserve your hands!'

INDEX

Abdine, 18
Abu el Haggag, 75
Abu Kir (church), 21
Abu Sarga (church), 21
Abu Simbel, 99, 100, 101
Abydos, 67, 68, 71
Ahmed ibn Tulun, 23
Akhenaten, 36, 40, 65, 79, 86
Albert (Lake), 62
Alexander, 106, 110, 111
Alexandria, 4, 6, 61, 108, 110, 111
Amenophis II, 86
Amenophis III, 36, 40, 74, 77
Amenophis IV (see Akhenaten)
Amon, 40
Amun, 33, 36, 73, 74, 75, 77, 101, 106
Amr ibn el As, 23
Antony, 111
Anubis, 35, 41, 45
Apis, 53, 54, 56
Assiut, 66
Aswan, 62, 88, 92, 100
Aswan (High Dam), 6, 94
Aten, 36
Atum, 33, 40
Ayun Mussa, 105

Bab el Futtuh, 25
Bab el Nasr, 25
Bab el Sharia, 18
Bab Zuweila, 25
Baharieh, 58
Bairam (Great), 17
Boulak, 18, 29

Caesar, 7
Cairo, 4, 8, 10, 12, 15, 17, 18, 19, 24, 45, 48, 61
Champollion (J.-F.), 29, 51
Cheops, 29, 45, 47, 50, 53, 71, 106
Chephren, 29, 45, 46
Clement of Alexandria, 115
Cleopatra, 6, 111, 115

Damietta, 108
Deir Abu Makar (monastery), 59
Deir Abu Sefein (monastery), 21
Deir Amba Baramos (monastery), 59
Deir Amba Bishoi (monastery), 59
Deir el Bahari, 78, 83
Deir el Medineh, 78, 81, 82, 83
Deir es Suriyan (monastery), 59, 61
Deir Mari Mina (monastery), 21
Dendera, 42, 65, 71
Djoser, 53
Dra Abu el Naga, 78

Edfu, 42, 48, 91
El Adrah (church), 21
El Alamein, 108
El Azhar (mosque), 6, 25
Elephantine (island), 92
El Harranieh, 109
El Katai, 24
El Moallaqah (church), 21
El Tahrir (bridge), 15, 17
Esna, 42, 91

Farafra, 58
Fayum, 64
Fustat, 24

Gabal Ahmar, 25
Garden City, 19
Geb, 38, 40
Gebel Mussa, 105
Gezira, 15, 17
Giza, 45, 48, 50, 51, 58
Gurnah, 78, 79, 116
Gurnet Murrai, 78

Hadrian, 111
Hapi, 91
Hassan (mosque), 6, 25
Hathor, 31, 35, 38, 71, 83, 94, 101
Hatshepsut, 73, 78, 85
Heb Sed, 33
Heliopolis, 10, 12, 19, 31, 40, 42
Heracleopolis, 59
Hermopolis, 34
Horemheb, 74, 86
Horus, 19, 31, 35, 45, 68, 91
Hurghada, 102
Hyksos, 31

Ibn Tulun (mosque), 6, 24
Imhotep, 51, 56
Isis, 31, 38, 94, 99
Ismailia, 104

Jawhar, 25

Kaaper, 29
Kalabsha, 99
Kalaum (mosque), 25
Karnak, 48, 73, 74, 116
Karun (Lake), 64
Keneh, 102
Khan el Khalili, 9, 12, 25, 116
Khargeh-Dakhleh, 58
Kheprer, 35
Khepri, 35
Kheri Aha, 19, 24
Khnum, 91
Kom Abu Billu, 59
Kom-Ombo, 97
Kosseir, 102

Luxor, 48, 65, 73, 74, 75, 91, 116

Maat, 41
Mameluks, 25
Manyal (Palace), 19
Mariette, 29
Mariut (Lake), 110
Medinet Habu, 83
Mehemet Ali, 25, 29
Mehemet Ali (mosque), 25
Memnon, 77

Memnon (colossi), 76
Memphis, 29, 42, 48, 53, 56
Menes, 6, 48, 56
Mennefru, 56
Mersa Matruh, 106
Midan el Tahrir (square), 12, 17, 26
Misr, 23
Mit Rahinah, 56
Montu (temple), 73
Moses, 105
Mukattam, 12, 24, 25, 46
Museums:
    Coptic (Cairo), 22
    Egyptian Museum of Antiquities (Cairo), 15,
        26, 29, 33
Mutemuia, 77
Mykerinos, 46

Nasser, 67, 99
Nasser (Lake), 97
Nectanebo, 94
Nefertari, 99, 100, 101
Nefretiti, 36, 65
Nekha Bit, 31, 33
Nephtis, 38
Nile, 4, 9, 12, 15, 18, 23, 26, 31, 35, 48, 58, 62,
    73, 75, 76, 80, 88, 91, 97, 116
Nile (Delta), 47, 108, 109
Nubia, 61, 92, 97
Nufreh, 29
Nun, 40
Nut, 38, 40

Omar, 23
Opet, 73, 74
Origen, 115
Osiris, 6, 31, 33, 35, 46, 53, 68, 79, 94

Pepi I, 56, 71
Per Hapi en Iun, 20
Philae, 42, 94
Philo, 115
Plotinus, 111, 115
Pompey (Pillar), 113
Porphyrius, 111
Port Said, 8, 104
Ptah, 53, 56, 73, 101
Ptahhotep (mastaba), 51
Ptolemies, 64, 71, 91, 108, 111
Pyramids:
    Pyramids of Giza, 45, 48
    Pyramid of Meidum, 53
    Rhomboidal Pyramid of Dashur, 52
    Step Pyramid of Djoser, 48, 50, 51

Qaitbai (mausoleum), 25
Qasr el Nil (street), 15
Qasr el Shamah, 20, 23

Ramesses, 9, 53, 56, 68, 74, 77, 99, 100
Ramesses III, 82, 83
Ramesseum, 77, 79
Ramoseh, 79, 116
Re, 33, 40, 46, 50, 59, 77, 85
Rodah, 12, 20

St Catherine (monastery), 105
St George (church), 21
St Jeremy (monastery), 50, 58
St Theodore the Oriental (cloister), 21
Sakkara, 9, 48, 51, 53, 54, 62, 64, 79
Saladin, 6, 12, 25

Saleh Talai (mosque), 25
Sayeda Zeinab, 18
Sebennytos, 38
Senenmut, 85
Sennedjem, 83
Sennufer, 86
Sesostris, 64
Set, 6, 19, 31, 33, 35, 54, 68
Sethi I, 68
Shamm en Nessim, 17
Shari el Galaa, 15
Sheikh el Beled, 29
Shemmis, 38
Shu, 40
Shubra, 18
Sinai, 104
Sitt Barbara (church), 21
Siwa, 58, 106
Snefru, 46, 53
Soleh, 35
Sphinx of Giza, 45
Sudan, 92
Suez, 8, 102, 104
Suez Canal, 103

Tell el Amarna, 36, 65
Thebes, 36, 40, 42, 56, 73, 74, 77, 78, 81, 88,
    116
Thinites, 68
Thoth, 33, 34, 38, 41, 45
Tiy, 56
Tiy (mastaba), 54, 62
Tiyi, 36, 40, 77
Tutankhamun, 26, 33, 74, 85, 86
Tuthmosis I, 85
Tuthmosis II, 45, 85
Tuthmosis III, 73, 82, 85

Usimareh, 77

Victoria (Lake), 62

Wadi es Sebwah, 99, 104
Wadi Natrun, 58, 59, 61
Waqfs, 24

729114

PHOTOGRAPHS

M. Abeille, 92
P. Bérenger (Top), 125 above
P. Boucas (Rapho), 7
J. Bulmer, 110, 114, 115
R. Burri (Magnum), 4–5, 79 above, 95, 102–103
J.-P. Charbonnier (Top), 23, 48–49, 91
G. Cranham (Rapho), 75
M. Desjardins (Top), 66, 66–67, 67, 83 above,
    96
R. Depardon (Gamma), 8
Explorer, 102
J. Fourment, 59, 88–89
L. Frédéric (Rapho), 101 above
M. Garanger, 12, 14, 15, 22, 46, 54, 57
M. Garanger (Giraudon), 124
G. Gerster (Rapho), 109
Giraudon, 125 below, 126 above
L. Goldman (Rapho), 105
H. Gougaud, 80, 81
Hassia, 10–11, 28, 29, 30, 33, 34, left, 35 right,
    36, 37, 39, 40–41, 41, 42, 43, 44, 53, 64, 65,
    70, 73, 77, 82, 90, 106, 107, 116–117
Keystone, 9
F. Lamy (Top), 51
Ch. Lenars, 32, 63
E. Lessing (Magnum), 79 below
The Louvre, 126 below
Marthelot (Afrique Photo), 56, 111
A. M. Picou (Afrique Photo), 78 above
Picture Point, 45
Raccah (photo Hachette), 52
Rapho, 71
E. Revault, 6, 17, 25, 58, 60, 61, 62 above
J. G. Ross (Rapho), 18 below, 47
H. W. Silvester (Rapho), 13, 68–69, 78 below
Ch. Simonpietri (Gamma), 16–17
P. Tetrel, 18 above, 18–19, 20 left, 20 right, 21,
    24, 26–27, 31, 34 right, 38, 50–51, 55, 62
    below, 72, 74, 76, 83 below, 84–85, 85, 86,
    86–87, 93, 97, 100, 101 below, 104, 108, 112,
    113 left, 113 right
Unesco, 94, 98, 99